SHOTGUNNING
for DEER
Guns, Loads, and Techniques for the Modern Hunter

Skyhorse Publishing books may be purchased in bulk at special discounts for sales promotion, corporate gifts, fund-raising, or educational purposes. Special editions can also be created to specifications. For details, contact the Special Sales Department, Skyhorse Publishing, 307 West 36th Street, 11th Floor, New York, NY 10018 or info@skyhorsepublishing.com.

Skyhorse® and Skyhorse Publishing® are registered trademarks of Skyhorse Publishing, Inc.®, a Delaware corporation.

www.skyhorsepublishing.com

10 9 8 7 6 5 4 3 2 1

Library of Congress Cataloging-in-Publication Data is available on file.
ISBN: 978-1-61608-416-5

Printed in China

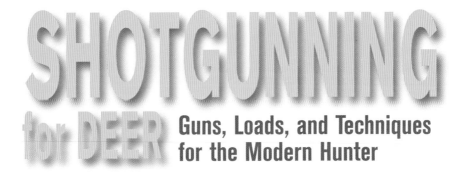

SHOTGUNNING for DEER
Guns, Loads, and Techniques for the Modern Hunter

Dave Henderson

Skyhorse Publishing

Contents

shotgunning for deer

About 4 million out of the country's 10 million whitetail deer hunters carry a shotgun when they go afield.

foreword

The most complete information comes from specialists. Specialists know not only what they say and write but things they don't say and write. Specialists know more than they have time or space to share, so they sift out what's not important. What you get is not just part of what they know, but the most important part. The stuff you don't get is woven into background that helps you understand what you do get.

Dave Henderson is a specialist. For as long as I've known him (decades!), he's focused his studies and his energies on hunting whitetail deer with shotguns. He has written more about slug shooting than anyone I know, and he writes from experience. While I've published hundreds of articles and several books about rifles, ballistics, and hunting, I don't hesitate to telephone Dave when a question comes up about shotgunning for deer. He's not just a specialist; he's the specialist. OK.

Part of the reason Dave gets the call is that he's easy to talk with. People who know the most seldom wear it on their sleeve. Dave Henderson has an easygoing style that comes through in his writing. He smiles when he talks, and you can feel that smile on the page. He likes what he does, and he writes about it as if he likes you too. As do all specialists, Dave studies history. History gives depth to understanding. A firm grasp of history is the underpinning of good advice. You'll find history here — enough to ground you in slug shooting, enough to make you an expert, perhaps enough to infect you with the same level of passion Dave Henderson brings to his writing.

Development of rifled shotgun barrels, powerful sabot slug loads and scopes especially for slug guns have fueled a boom in shotgunning for deer. First by regulation and now often by choice, whitetail hunters have left their rifles at home. New shotguns and loads boast twice the reach they had in the 1960s, when in my native Michigan hunters were still scoring paper hulls with a pocketknife to make "cut shells" for hunting deer. Dave Henderson was hunting then, and he'll take you back there. More importantly, he'll bring you into the present, with sound technical information, advice on hunting and shooting, and entertaining anecdotes from his many hunts. There are other useful books on hunting. But if you hunt deer with a shotgun, you must read this one. It's that good. It's written by the specialist.

— Wayne van Zwoll

The Ithaca Model 37 and Browning BPS

To Dad: Now that I understand all that stuff you told me, I only wish you were here to share it.

— Dave Henderson

preface

I read 'em all while growing up — Jack O'Connor, Warren Page, Elmer Keith, Col. Askins, et al. I couldn't wait for their next magazine articles. But to a jug-eared country kid in the Northeast, 400-yard shots with a .270 across a windswept drainage for Dall sheep, or toppling a charging cape buffalo with a .458 were about as close to reality as an inter-planetary space trip with Buck Rogers. Possessed early on with the sense that the Mickey Mantles, Willie Mays and Jim Browns of the world were extraordinary beings who, like the famous gun writers, also lived on a different plane; the figures that I chose to emulate were of a more corporeal sort. Living in shotgun country, my heroes were deer hunters — Dad and my uncles. My "big game" dreams centered not around Persian rams or high-country elk, but rather around getting an open 50-yard (or closer) shot at a standing whitetail. Any size rack would do. In fact, antlers weren't even a prerequisite in those deer-scarce days.

In fact, those aspirations guided my very being on March 25, 1963, as birthday presents lay before me on the tattered rug of our living room floor. Socks, a shirt, a pair of Wranglers and the bone-handled jackknife I'd lusted after so long in the hardware store window. I'd also gotten the day off from milking the neighbor's Holsteins. Given the times and our station in life, I certainly didn't expect the fourteenth anniversary of my birth to afford me anything more. Then Dad brought a long box in from the truck. "Here's another one," said Dad, never one for suspense. The box was plain and the return address of Ithaca, New York, meant nothing to a curious country kid. I tore it open. The contents were wrapped in heavy brown paper, the inner layers of which were stained with grease. As soon as I saw the barrel I knew what it was. Ithaca Gun's Model 66 was a Plain-Jane, lever-action, break-action single-shot 20-gauge. It was a popgun by today's standards, and not an elephant gun even back then, but it was a shotgun. My shotgun.

"You're old enough to hunt now and you'll need your own gun," said Dad, his voice, barely perceptible to my adrenaline-addled mind. "Look at me now," came Dad's stern admonition, "I want you to realize that guns are made for one thing — to kill things. They don't know or care what they kill. They're just a tool and it's up to the man to use it right. It's always loaded, even when you know there's nothing in it. It's never safe. You are the only thing that can keep it from killing. This thing can kill you; it can kill me; it can kill Mom, or your brother or somebody you don't even know. It's up to you to keep that from happening." When Dad spoke, you listened. He was a loving but forceful man who could get his point across with a look and a vice-like grip on a young arm. He spoke only when it meant something. A combat veteran in World War II, he came home from Europe with a Bronze Star and a couple of Purple Hearts that he would never talk about. I never heard him discuss world affairs, religion or the neighbors. He didn't waste words on the weather, politics or inane social greetings. But when he did talk, he expected your undivided attention and he certainly had mine at that moment.

"The fact that you're old enough to hunt scares the hell out of me," he said. "You're still a kid, but when you have a gun in your hands you've got to be a man and that's a tremendous responsibility. It's not a game. If you're careless somebody can get killed." He paused, probably for effect. His next words were measured and the message very clear. "Do you remember what happened with the bow?" he asked, referring to a spanking new fiberglass recurve that he'd crushed in his workshop vise two summers previously after seeing me carelessly shoot without first checking the whereabouts of my brother. "If I ever see you pointing this gun at something you don't intend to kill, I'll take it and you'll never hunt with us again." His voice tore through the excitement of the moment and hit home hard.

A lump formed in my throat and tears welled up in my eyes as I imagined the worst-case scenario. I went from total exhilaration to abject dread. Becoming accepted as a member of the family hunting clan was all I'd ever aspired to. Suddenly I envisioned losing that opportunity and the thought was terrifying. Dad's message remains etched in my consciousness these many decades later. That responsibility was intimidating at first. Toting that gun in Dad's presence, ever mindful of where the muzzle pointed; checking the safety and muzzle at every opportunity; watching other hunters' handling of their guns. It was all part of the lesson. And my performance wasn't perfect. More than once I tearfully marched through an afternoon of rabbit hunting with a gun emptied on demand because, after falling, I'd been too slow in checking the bore for snow. *("If you don't take care of your gun, your gun will take care of you.")* My uncles at times pleaded with Dad to lighten up on the kid, lest he "ruin hunting" for me. "That's better than him ruining his life or somebody else's," Dad would answer adamantly.

The author took this caribou with a Mossberg 500 Mariner pump gun and a Lightfield slug.

Dad's been gone nearly 40 years now but to this day I'm ever mindful of where gun muzzles are pointed and if the bore is clear. Hunting and shooting are virtually a daily routine but I still check chambers and safeties with religious vigor. I've missed countless opportunities at game because I won't disengage the safety until the gun is fully aimed or because I didn't load up until I was a sensible distance from the truck. Whenever I've got a gun in my hands I can hear Dad's voice. It's like he's still here, looking over my shoulder. It's still intimidating and I'm forever thankful for that.

— Dave Henderson

introduction

Who the hell is Dave Henderson? Well, the author would love to be described as a champion shooter, woodsman of uncanny ability and a sportsman of international renown. The truth of the matter, however, is that he is pretty much an ordinary guy who's lived a blessed life. Oh, he's a better than average shooter, but then he should be, considering the prodigious amount of ammunition he burns on a regular basis. As a former hunting guide, his woodsmanship is probably more than adequate, but he has also been known to shoot slow at bucks running fast; gets more respect from the B Division shooters than the AA boys and doesn't bring home the biggest buck in the county every year. In fact, he never has.

Even though he's found time to hunt in 30 different states and 10 Canadian provinces, he has spent far more time behind a desk than afield.

The author in his office.

The plaques on the wall are not awards for hunting or shooting but rather for writing about it with some degree of competence. He is, above all, a reporter. A good reporter is seldom an all-knowing expert on a topic but rather someone who knows where to find such an expert and translate that knowledge into readable prose. Suffice it to say that the author knows a lot of experts.

Please understand that during his formative days in this trade, all self-respecting journalists regretted the use of the personal pronoun. Times and journalistic outlooks have changed, but his hasn't. Apologies are offered, therefore, since the use of first person singular is simply unavoidable in a book like this. I have devoted the bulk of my professional life to researching and writing about shotgun hunting and this book is a manifestation of that personal quest. It comes from a guy who is well into his fourth decade as a professional journalist, having started out as a newspaper hack in upstate New York. Since becoming a full-time free lance writer in the 1980s, I've held dozens of editing and columnist positions in national and regional outdoors publications, most of them having to do with guns and hunting and many of them now defunct. Although I hunt and compete with bolt-action centerfire and muzzleloader rifles and occasionally with a bow, it's shotgunning that provides me with a means of gainful employment.

This is, in fact, my third book on the subject — a fourth having been on deer hunting — and I've contributed shotgun-hunting chapters to three others. I have no binding allegiances to organizations, causes or brand names but am familiar with them all as you will see in the pages that follow. If outside references are needed for a rounder picture, be advised that I am definitely not politically correct, drive only American vehicles and don't wear an earring. I've never played Nintendo, couldn't tell you which musical group sings what and don't feel culturally deprived when I work or sleep through television's prime-time hours. I'm addicted to caffeine, wear watches with hands and am still innocent enough to think of the beverage every time the word "coke" is dropped in casual conversation.

My spouse does not share my passion for guns or hunting but nevertheless understands better than most what it is that makes a man forsake a warm bed to face dawn in a windswept tree stand – and the need to keep a straight face when excuses abound for the latest missed shot. We live in a house where venison, wild birds and fish provide virtually all of the meat protein. I'm still on friendly terms with our daughter who, as an adult, now openly prefers wild meat after spending her teen years making faces at the table fare. Above all I have spent most of my adult life getting paid to do things that any sensible man would happily do for free. This book is simply an extension of that good fortune and I look forward to sharing it with you.

My professional journey has, however, been anything but a solo flight. Plenty of folks have contributed and need to be acknowledged. Russell Thornberry is a world-class human being who also gave me the first regular outlet for deer shotgun information when he was editor of *Buckmasters Whitetail Magazine*. Mike Jordan was one of the best ballistic minds in the business when he was with Winchester-Olin and was always able – and willing – to share that knowledge in laymen's terms. Rich Knoster of Pennsylvania is a friend and one of the co-founders of the Slug Group that kindled and fanned interest in slug shooting just as it began its meteoric leap forward in the early 1990s. The Slug Group and some of Rich's other innovations are gone now but nevertheless provided me with ideas and support for many years.

Fellow writers Don Zutz, Bryce Towsley, Wayne van Zwoll, John Barsness, John Weiss, Jim Carmichel, Jon Sundra and John Taylor contributed by way of their printed work, which I have long used for reference. The late Don Zutz, one of the best shotgun minds ever, encouraged me to write this book when I kept putting it off in the late 1990s, because I felt that it would be instantly outdated by the constant flow of new technology. In fact, the book eventually headed down several other publishing avenues, all of which ended up as dead ends and I was ready to self-publish it when old friend Jay Langston, a graduate of the magazine and gun writing ranks, moved into the publisher's chair at Stoeger Publications. Jay immediately saw the potential for this book, encouraged me and patiently waited for its delivery.

The guy who has contributed most and most often to my life in shotgunning is Randy Fritz. You'll find the engaging Pennsylvania gunmaker-ballistics expert mentioned and quoted frequently throughout this book, as should be the case since he is undoubtedly the preeminent mind on slug shooting in this universe. I like to think I know a lot about slug shooting but every time I spend a session with Randy I come away with something new on the subject. Randy's been a friend, an ally and advisor from the Slug Group days through countless load-testing, gun-building, video-making and hotel-room or show-booth bull sessions – all much to my benefit.

Thanks bud.

— Dave Henderson

The all-copper Improved Remington Copper Solid and copper-clad Federal Barnes EXpander slugs.

Why Use a Shotgun?

shotgunning for deer

The New York State record typical buck — once the world record -- was taken in 1939 with a punkin ball slug fired from a shotgun.

Next page:
The author cautiously approaches a fallen buck taken with a slug gun. Most shotgun hunters select slugs as their ammunition of choice.

Hunting deer with a shotgun is a lot like going to bat in a baseball game with a broomstick. Both implements may be used somewhat effectively, but neither represents the most efficient nor preferred method. As suburbia continues its relentless expansion into deer habitat and humans and whitetails compete increasingly for elbowroom, more and more munici-palities are mandating shotguns for big game hunting rather than permitting the use of long-range modern rifles. This is not to say that shotguns are not effective for deer hunting. In fact, the largest-grossing typical whitetail buck recorded in the history of the Boone & Crockett Club's scoring system was taken by an Illinois shotgun hunter in 1993. The two largest bucks taken in the history of my native New York, a 198-plus typical and a 267-plus nontypical, were both killed during the 1930s with old "punkin ball" slugs.

Today about 4.1 million of the nation's 10 million whitetail hunters go afield armed with shotguns, and the number is growing every year. More than 20 states mandate the use of shotguns for deer for at least some of their hunters. Eight states limit all of their hunters to shotguns or muzzleloaders for deer. Delaware, Massachusetts, New Jersey and Rhode Island allow buckshot or slugs while Illinois, Indiana, Iowa and Ohio limit everyone to slugs. Connecticut used to prohibit rifles but now allows them for hunting on holdings larger than 10 acres, with written permission from the landowner. Eight other states limit at least 40 percent of their hunters to slugs and/or buckshot. Pennsylvania, historic home of the American rifle, now restricts more than 100,000 of its hunters to slug guns and muzzleloaders by mandating special regulations areas around Philadelphia and Pittsburgh. New York has nearly 400,000 slug shooters. Even such frontier outposts as Helena, Montana, and Edmonton, Alberta, have shotgun-only hunting areas in their outer suburbs.

At last count only about 3 percent of today's shotgun deer hunters must or opt to use buckshot; the rest use slugs of one form or another. Given a fast-growing market, development of slug loads and slug-shooting shotguns has advanced more in the last 20 years than any other aspect of the firearms industry. Today's high-velocity, high-tech sabot slugs and rifled barrel slug guns have turned shotgun deer hunting from a "wait-

Richard Paulli displays the mount of the Boone & Crockett 267-plus buck that he took with a shotgun in Illinois in 1983. It is still one of the largest scoring whitetail bucks taken with a slug.

'til-you-see-the-whites-of-their-eyes" proposition into an event where the hunter can no longer be faulted for preheating the oven when a rack appears a couple of hundred yards away. Regardless, being of sound mind and body, if I'm given a choice, I'll use a rifle for hunting deer rather than a shotgun. I thus found it surprising when, in my native New York, there was staunch opposition to a legislative proposal to allow rifles in the largely agricultural western portion of the state, which has been restricted to slug guns ever since deer hunting was regulated in the late 1930s.

There is obviously a core of deer hunters who are satisfied with shotguns for deer, but the majority of us who do hunt with a shotgun probably do so because we don't have any choice in the matter. Most of us do, however, have a choice of loads and guns, and given the recent boom in technology in this area, there are plenty of viable options. Which one is right for you? Let's take a look.

slugs or buckshot?

First of all, if you have a choice between buckshot and slugs, there is no choice. Slugs are absolutely the most effective load you can put into a shotgun. Granted, buckshot is a devastating close-range load. In fact, the

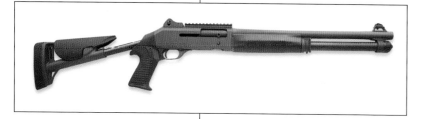

Shotguns are effective tactical weapons for the military and law enforcement personnel.

Germans complained to the Hague and Geneva Conventions regarding the shotgun's horrific effect in trench warfare during World War I. That's the reason shotguns were outlawed under the Law of Armed Conflict, Article 23, by the Hague Convention, a decree that the United States chose not to observe.

American armed forces used a variety of pump shotguns in the Pacific Theater during World War II, and later in Korea. While the distinctive patter of the M16 rifle was readily identifiable as an American presence, the lion's bellow of a 10-gauge pump loaded with double-aught buckshot may well have been the most feared sound in the up-close-and-personal jungle environs of Vietnam. Ithaca, Mossberg, Winchester and Remington all built tactical scatterguns for U.S. troops.

Buddy and fellow writer J. Wayne Fears says he favored the companionship of a Winchester 97 while serving in the jungles of Southeast Asia with U.S. Special Forces. Wayne said of the 97 that it was one gun you always knew whether it was ready or not, by the hammer position. Any slug, full-bore or sabot, 20-, 16-, 10- or 12-gauge, has a much, much more extensive effective range than buckshot in the same gauge and,

Modern sabot slugs shoot very flat and perform very well on deer-sized game.

although the margin for error is slightly less, is every bit as deadly in close quarters. But given the choice, the vast majority of American shotgunners will go with slugs every time.

types of slugs

Despite all of the hype about saboted ammunition that you read in magazines and see on television, the conventional full-bore slug still represents more than 60 percent of the retail sales to slug hunters. Does saboted ammunition have a longer effective range? Definitely. Is it more accurate when fired from a rifled bore than full-bore slugs are from a smoothbore? Absolutely. Does everyone need that extra wallop and extended range? Nope. Longstanding (and somewhat outdated) surveys have shown that 97 percent of all deer killed with shotguns are taken at ranges of less than 100 yards. An impressive 94 percent are actually taken inside of 75 yards. Foster-type full-bore slugs, such as those loaded by Winchester, Federal and Remington and the various non-saboted Brenneke-style designs, are very effective at that range.

Buckshot is a very effective deer hunting load when used at limited ranges.

If you shoot a smoothbore shotgun and take typical shots within these parameters, you are not at a disadvantage with full-bore slugs. Saboted ammunition, at least before the new high-velocity stuff hit the mar-

An extraordinary array of shotgun slugs are available to modern deer hunters.

ket, offered little advantage over full-bore slugs at traditional deer hunting ranges (40-80 yards). The high-tech ammunition didn't really show its stuff until it had a chance to stretch out and run at longer distances. At that point the high-tech ammunition's superior aerodynamics and ballistic coefficient and the stabilizing effect of the spin generated by the rifling helped the projectile maintain its velocity, trajectory and energy over a greater distance than did the bulky full-bore slug.

Foster-type rifled slugs and the 2 ³/₄-inch Brenneke smoothbore slugs look essentially the same as they did when they were introduced – *(Foster's in 1933 and the Original Brenneke in 1935)* – but have undergone some subtle improvements over the years. For instance, Winchester redesigned its Double-X load in 1982 by swelling the diameter to fill all bores and by making it more consistently concentric. Federal Cartridge followed with a redesign in 1985 and again in the early 1990s while Remington finally swelled the diameter and made some changes to its venerable Slugger in 1993.

ORIGINAL BRENNEKE   FOSTER

Today's Original Brenneke slug and the Foster-style rifled slug (loaded by Winchester, Remington and Federal) are visually identical to their original 1930s prototypes.

barrels make a difference

What about chokes for slug shooting? Odds are that your smoothbore will shoot a slug more accurately with a relatively open choke. The industry, in fact, used to suggest improved cylinder for slug shooting. But shotgun bores vary in dimension, bore to bore, even in the same brand and model. A slug that has been squeezed tightly throughout its journey down the barrel will react differently when it hits the choke – regardless of the constriction of that choke – than one that fits loosely and tipped slightly as it traversed the same distance. I've seen some modified choke shotguns that were real tack drivers and the post-war Belgian Browning Auto-5 that I inherited from Dad shot Brennekes like they were designed for each other – despite its fixed full-choke barrel.

Will shooting high-tech sabot loads through your smoothbore increase your effective range? Maybe, but certainly not to the point that would justify paying 7 or 8 times as much as you would for full-bore slugs. In fact, you will find that saboted ammunition is less effective in a smoothbore than conventional slugs since, if the slug is not spinning, the sabot sleeves will have difficulty separating from the slug and will actually destabilize the projectile. Sabot slugs are designed for rifled barrels; the soft material of the sabot sleeves grips the rifling and imparts spin to the projectile, which it needs to maintain stability. Full-bore slugs rely on a nose-heavy design for stability during a relatively short flight.

If you shoot a smoothbore but would like to take advantage of the high-tech loads, your best bet is to add a rifled choke tube. All major shotgun manufacturers offer rifled tubes and they are improving all the time. You can also look into aftermarket tubes from Hastings, Colonial, Cation and others – The length of the choke tube is a factor in how well it stabilizes slugs. After all, asking 2 to 3 inches of spiraled grooves to impart a rotation of up to 37,000 rpm on a projectile that has already reached terminal velocity is

Knowing what loads are designed for what type of shotgun barrels makes a difference in the deer woods.

asking a lot. Regardless, I've seen some rifled tubes that shot far more accurately, particularly inside of 100 yards, than the laws of physics should allow.

The fact remains, however, if you want to take advantage of the latest innovations and vast ballistic superiority of today's high-tech slugs, you'll need a rifled slug barrel. Be advised that a rifled barrel dedicates the gun to slug shooting only, it will not effectively pattern shot. It will, however, stabilize any slugs — sabot or full-bore Foster or Brenneke-style — and extend their effective range. In fact, full-bore slugs actually skid a bit in the rifling and leave copious amounts of lead fouling in the grooves in a very short period of time, but they will shoot well in a rifled bore. The best slug gun models will have fixed rifled barrels, which means they can't be used for anything but slug shooting, unlike models with interchangeable barrels. As with rifled choke tubes, all major shotgun manufacturers offer at least one model with a rifled barrel and most offer optional rifled barrels that can replace your conventional barrel for the deer season.

With a stiff barrel, good trigger and solidly mounted scope your rifled barrel slug gun should be able to consistently put three conventional-velocity saboted slugs through the same hole at 50 yards from a solid rest. Accuracy at 100 yards will vary with the wind conditions, trigger pull, load and the shooter's ability. To sum it up, what you need from a slug gun depends entirely on how you are going to use it. There's nothing wrong with smoothbore shotguns and full-bore slugs for the relatively short ranges encountered in most deer woods. If you're looking for long-range performance in your slug gun, however, that option is available in rifled-barrel shotguns and high-tech saboted ammunition.

Rifle-sights or optics are a necessity for a slug gun. Slug shooting is a specialty use of a shotgun — you must aim the gun rather than just point it.

More than 60 percent of whitetail deer hunters choose smoothbore shotguns and use full-bore (non-sabot) slugs.

Evolution of the Shotgun Slug
then and now

FOSTER SLUG BEFORE FIRING

FOSTER SLUG AFTER FIRING

The Foster-style slug, before and after it has been fired into ballistic gelatin, a composition which approximates the mass and density of a deer carcass.

Next page:
The author with the Illinois buck taken with the Lightfield Commander slug and Tar-Hunt custom slug gun.

Shivering against the late November cold, I pulled the Woolrich's long collar tight around my neck and flattened my scrawny teen-aged form even tighter against the lee side of the giant beech that served as both backrest and windbreak. Getting a "stander's" position on a deer drive was a rare occurrence for a kid with a short but bleak history of missing deer and I wasn't going to let discomfort interfere with this rare opportunity. Just then I caught sight of movement in the periphery of my vision. Three deer were racing across the snow-covered hayfield toward the woodlot in which I was situated. I realized that they'd probably enter the trees at a point about 70 yards away, and would likely still be sprinting. My shaking hands pointed the Ithaca 66's Raybar bead toward an opening I felt they'd pass through. I didn't even have the hammer back on the 20-gauge single-shot when the first brown form flashed through the sight picture. I lined up the sights just as the second flashed by and was pressing the heavy trigger when the last form hit the opening – BANG!

The deer, three dark forms against the snow-covered woodlot floor, bounded out of sight, leaving the woods silent except for the ringing in my ears. Failure. I'd missed – again! Not an unfamiliar feeling but certainly a discouraging one. Crestfallen over the most recent failure, I disobeyed the ironclad order to never leave a stand during a drive, walking disconsolately down to check the tracks and see if I could find the slug's furrow in the snow. Whoa! Blood. There was a spray of blood and hair on the snow. I found more there and more. Lying just 60 yards away in thick brush was my first deer, an unlucky spike who'd run into the wrong place at the wrong time, taking $5/8$ of an ounce of soft lead through the lungs.

Fast forward nearly four decades and I'm watching a steep grassy hillside below a browned Illinois CRP field on a chilly November morning when a strange object sails over the hilltop. I don't realize what it is until the buck lands on the hillside and sprints downhill toward the perceived sanctuary of the wooded creek bottom to my left. I've got a split second to evaluate his rack, get the gun up and take aim before he reaches the trees at the bottom of the hill. Judging the distance at about 100 yards, I get the sprinting form in the scope, swing the crosshairs ahead of his chest and trip the 2.5-pound trigger, ever mindful to keep the barrel swinging. In

Prior to the 1930's shotgun, "punkin ball" slugs were simply sub-gauge round balls loaded into a standard paper hull.

a feeling born of experience, I'm confident of the sight picture and familiar trigger pull and am rewarded with a loud crashing sound in the trees where he'd disappeared.

I find the big 9-pointer suspended in two splintered saplings where he'd died in mid-stride just 25 yards from where the slug had struck him. The 12-gauge, 600-grain Lightfield Commander, typical of today's high-velocity, very accurate slugs, is light-years ahead of the 5/8-ounce, 20-gauge Foster-style slug that I used to kill my first deer 37 years previously. In fact, looking back I'm amazed that my 1960's shot was fatal. The contemporary Lightfield struck, at 100 yards, with a force of nearly 2,000 foot-pounds while the 1964 slug probably had less than 600 pounds left when it found its target at 70 yards. Comparing 1960's vintage slugs with today's state-of-the-art high-velocity projectiles is like juxtaposing the Wright brothers' Kitty Hawk flying machine and the Space Shuttle.

major transition

Those of us with at least a little gray at the temples can remember when slug shooting was an entirely different proposition. In my early years (the 1950-60s) of slug shooting virtually everyone used their rabbit guns for deer hunting — they simply changed the loads. You sort of pointed slug guns in those days instead of aiming. Dad bought slugs of mixed brands at a hardware store bin at 9 cents apiece. He'd buy 10 new ones every year, use several from last year for practice and hunt with the new stuff. We paid very little attention to brand, bore sizes, or even chokes. Accuracy, of course, was problematical.

It wasn't so long ago that hunters changed their shotguns from rabbit guns to deer guns by simply changing the loads.

Accuracy is and has always been a relative term. In those days a shotgun that would put three of five shots into a gallon can at 40 paces was considered a tack driver. Writer Gary Sitton once said of those days that if you could put five straight slugs in a coffee can at 100 yards you could start your own religion. Today my slug gun is a custom bolt-action with a Jewell trigger, synthetic stock and heavy, rifled (gain twist) barrel made of 4140 rifle steel. It is capable of minute-of-angle accuracy at 100 yards. Certainly slug guns have advanced mightily over the last three decades but not nearly as far as the loads. The fact that my current gun is lethal at nearly 200 yards (under the right conditions) has more do to the slugs — actually large-bore pistol bullets encased in a bore-filing plastic sleeve — than the launcher.

debunking slug myths

Slugs have taken a quantum leap forward since the 1980s. So much so that magazine articles and supposed experts will point out that today's high-

velocity, controlled expansion, 200-yard, bullet-style slugs – the Winchester Partition Gold, Platinum Tip, DualBond and XP3, Hornady SST, Federal's high-velocity Barnes Expander, Fusion and Tipped Barnes Expander and Remington's Core-Lokt Ultra and Accu-Tip – eclipse the venerable .45-70, .300 Savage, .30-30 and other elderly centerfire calibers. On paper, that's true, but we don't hunt on paper. In fact, the worries flew early in the high-velocity revolution that the gaudy slug ballistics might cause some hunting regulation-makers to rethink what is allowable in shotgun-only areas.

Actually, there shouldn't be any worry if those decision makers are well informed. "Rifle bullets and shotgun slugs are very different animals," Chub Eastman told me late in his career with Nosler Bullets. "We are doing some impressive things with slugs but the ballistic coefficient is so low *(Winchester Partition Gold 20-gauge is 0.1991)* that it's like shooting pencil erasers when you compare them to rifle bullets." Consider that a conventional shotgun slug has a maximum range of less than 900 yards, and that's when it's fired from a barrel elevated 30 degrees. Your .30-06 will carry more than three miles from the same position. A 10 mph crosswind will move a conventional shotgun slug 6 - 8 inches off target at 100 yards. A 130-grain bullet from a .270 fired from the same bench under the same conditions will move about an eighth of an inch.

Shotguns and slugs are short-range ordnance, regardless of what you've read. Modern high-velocity shotgun slugs are effec-

These Ohio deer hunters are limited to shotguns, but that doesn't seem to be a liability.

Slug shooting has taken a quantum leap forward in effectiveness and accuracy over the last 25 years.

DEER CARTRIDGES   SLUGS

Despite huge technological advances, slugs remain short-range projectiles that will never perform like conventional centerfire deer cartridges.

Rifled slugs, such as the Foster type shown here, do not spin when fired. Their effectiveness is due to a nose-heavy design combined with a hollow point to increase expansion.

Karl Foster patterned his rifled shotgun slug after the Civil War-era Minié ball rifle round *(left)*, producing a nose-heavy design with a concave rear and thin skirts that flared at ignition to seal the bore.

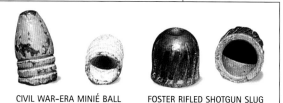

CIVIL WAR-ERA MINIÉ BALL   FOSTER RIFLED SHOTGUN SLUG

tive, under the right conditions, with the right shooter, out to 125 yards. An expert might stretch it to 150 or 160 under the right conditions but once you get much beyond 125, luck has far more influence on the results than do ballistics. While we're at it, let's set the record straight on two myths associated with slugs. "Rifled" slugs are not spun by the grooves on their body, although manufacturers would like you to continue thinking in that vein, and all of the power ascribed to slugs as a result of "hydrostatic shock" on impact is pretty much bullfeathers too.

Hydrostatic shock is the lethal effect of a literal shock wave flashing through an animal's body in the wake of a high-velocity projectile. The shock causes tissue damage and trauma far from the actual wound cavity, called cavitation. The trouble is that it is a widely held contention among ballisticians that hydrostatic shock does not take place in the case of projectiles moving slower than 2,000 fps and conventional slugs don't come close to that threshold. The personal feeling is that the phenomenon's velocity level may well be closer to 1,800 fps since I have seen several deer felled instantly by nonskeletal hits from the 1,800-fps Winchester Partition Gold. Conventional velocity slugs do not, however, convey hydrostatic shock, as long claimed. Regardless, the new stuff may not threaten rifle performance but it's virtually light-years ahead of yesterday's slugs.

history of slugs

The origins of shotgunning for deer are unclear. In researching my book, *The Ultimate Guide to Shotgunning*, I found that the practice probably had it origins in the 13th or 14th century. Early guns were simply containment tubes that held powder and multiple-piece loads of whatever sinister small, hard and pointed items were handy. The practice of shooting a single ball or bullet through a smoothbore evolved when the need arose to take down standing targets at longer ranges. Rifled bores suitable for single-ball loads appeared in the late 1400s but rifles weren't commonplace until more than two centuries later. But at what point did the smoothbore stop being a musket and become a shotgun? Lightweight fowling pieces, probably the first dedicated shotguns, were introduced for bird hunting during the late 17th century and musket and trade gun wielding hunters in colonial North America used buck-and-ball combinations or a tight-fitting lead ball as early hunting loads. In the early days of tiger hunting in India and Nepal, British sportsmen used buckshot to great advantage before turning to bore-fitting iron slugs that "killed like hell."

The shotgun slug was and is a simple example of brute force that trades precision for devastating energy. In the 1880s, however, a "de-evolution" of sorts came about in slug shooting when choked shotgun barrels became the rage. Choke constriction was a definite drawback for early slug shooters. Made smaller than bore diameter to squeeze and tighten a shot charge, chokes would not let a full-bore slug pass, a factor that caused manufacturers to label choked guns "not for ball." The result was that the slugs of the era were made smaller so that they could pass through a choked muzzle. In fact, they were made much smaller to accommodate all degrees of choke.

Early 1900s 12-gauge balls were commonly cast from .645 of an inch to .660 for passage down bores that were approximately .730 inch. A 12-gauge slug was commonly less than an ounce in weight and typically would roll down a 16-gauge bore unimpeded. One can imagine accuracy of the "punkin balls" as they were called. They were pretty much 30- to 40-yard loads unless they were loaded with a bore-fitting cloth patch. Not many shotgunners went to the trouble of swaddling punkin balls in cloth, however, and instead opted for buckshot. Nevertheless, the impact of a bore-fitting, well-placed single ball was much more effective than a charge of buckshot propelled by the same amount of powder, and hunters of the day continually looked for an improved punkin ball.

For most of the 20th century, shotgun slug design followed one of the patterns shown above. The standard sub-gauge round, or "punkin ball," was followed by *(left to right)* the Foster slug in the 1930s, the BRI sabot slug in the 1960s and the Barnes X-bullet by 1995.

karl foster's innovation

In the early 1930s independent ballistic researcher and inveterate hunter Karl Foster of Great Barrington, Massachusetts, effectively turned shotguns into modern-day muskets with a slug design that emulated the Minié ball that shot so well in Civil War-era blackpowder rifles. Records show that early in the slug's development, Foster made a "breakthrough" when he was able to put 10 of his 20-gauge slugs in a 10-inch circle at 50 yards. At one point he spent an entire day filing "rifling" grooves into six slugs in order to impart a rifle-like spin to them. He would later find that they didn't spin, but taking a 180-pound buck with one kept his interest keen. At one point he had Lyman make him some 12- and 16-gauge molds that added curved longitudinal grooves to the surface of the slugs. His slug design, however, was rejected after a test by Remington technicians in Bridgeport, Connecticut, in 1932 and later by Winchester-Western in New Haven.

While the technicians did note improved accuracy over round balls, they were not sufficiently impressed to recommend the new slugs for production. But Foster stayed with his research, supplied local hunters with his loads, and by 1935 another version of the slug with a heavier nose thickness was averaging 5-inch groups at 50 yards and Winchester-Western bought the idea. It's been said that the man who convinced New Haven to look at the newer Foster design was Major Jack Hessions, a former Wimbledon Cup champion and influential Winchester devotee who

BEFORE FIRING   WITHIN TARGET

The Foster slug's effectiveness as a short-range deer round is largely due to its molecular cohesiveness — it retains its mass while deforming in the target.

For decades the Foster slug was manufactured at well under the bore diameters for which it was intended, a feature that compromised its performance.

Foster had kept supplied with slugs throughout the research and development. The Foster-style slug debuted on the market as a 16-gauge in 1936 and shortly thereafter Remington brought out its own version.

By then all slugs were swaged – forced into a mold by pressure rather than cast. Basically Foster's design was a molded nose-heavy lead cup with skirts that flared upon ignition to fill the bore and the Foster-style slug took over the market in the years following World War II and today – loaded by Winchester, Federal and Remington in 10-, 12-, 16-, 20- and even .410-gauge – still serves as the best seller nationwide. They are called "rifled slugs" because of the aforementioned curved longitudinal grooves or flutes swaged into the outside walls. A ballistician once confided in me that the main purpose of the grooves or flutes was to give the surface a buffer or raised portion that would be squeezed down in a tight choke without disturbing the actual body of the slug. Rifling also adds a modicum of sales appeal, he said.

The slug is stabilized in flight by its nose-heavy design, the center of gravity is placed in front of the center of pressure much the same as a badminton shuttlecock. Put a rock in a sock and throw it, you'll see how it works. The forward, heavy center of gravity tends to keep that end pointed downrange. Compared to a bullet, the Foster slug has a highly inefficient shape, heavy weight and low velocity – but it stood as a vast improvement over punkin balls. Short and soft, the Foster slug sheds as much as 50 percent of its energy in the first 50 yards but is effective on deer-sized game at short range because its mass keeps driving it through tissue as it flattens. Its impressive molecular cohesiveness holds it together in soft tissue.

This fired Brenneke slug is made of harder metal and is designed to distribute its energy through the target by penetrating rather than expanding.

enter the brenneke

Better yet were the unique, heavy, bore-sized slugs that German Wilhelm Brenneke's shop had been producing since 1898. Brenneke introduced an elongated lead projectile with a bore diameter compatible with either choke or cylinder-bored guns. The theory behind the German design was based on forward weight plus a bearing surface utilizing overall length, ribs and grooves. In addition to providing bearing surface in the tube, the ribs also became swaged as they moved through the choke constriction, protecting the integrity of the main body of the slug. The fact that the Brenneke is cast in bore-diameter while the Foster slugs were typically cast undersized relying on the expansion of the skirts to fill the bore (sealing gases behind), made the German slug more accurate and powerful. It was slightly modified over the years but the 2 3/4-inch, 12-gauge version with a three-part fiber wad attached to the rear of the slug with a flathead Phillips-head screw, is still called the "Original Brenneke" when loaded by Dynamit-Nobel (Rottweil) and has not changed appreciably since 1935.

The Brenneke's performance advantage over the Foster slug was that it was made larger than the bore diameter and had a long bearing surface, which sealed the gases behind it and kept it concentric in the bore.

The attached wad design is the basis for the majority of European and even some subsequent American slug designs, such as the Italian-made Gualandi and Cervo slugs and the American-designed Activ and Lightfield Hybred designs. The Gualandi shell is loaded by the Canadian manufacturer Challenger and by the tiny Nitro Company in Missouri. The Cervo is loaded by Fiocchi USA in Missouri and was formerly loaded by Activ and the now-defunct Dan Arms. Due to a couple of world wars, the German Brenneke didn't get much exposure in the United States until the 1950s. In fact, Brenneke's original factory in Leipzig was destroyed in World War II and the family was left with no male heirs when the company was resurrected in Berlin in 1946.

Today Brenneke is headed by Peter Manke, a son of Wilhelm Brenneke's daughter. Although there have been countless other European designs over the years — Boughnet, Berntheisel-Luneville, Witzleben, Kohler, Grenate, Stenebach, Andre-Charleroi and Vitt-Broos — none really caught on to any degree stateside. Today Brennekes — loaded in the U.S. by Dynamit-Nobel, Kent Cartridge and PMC as well as Brenneke USA — stand with the Fosters as the prime ordnance for smoothbore guns. The Foster slug's shape and poor ballistic coefficient *(about 0.060-0.075, depending on gauge, manufacturer, etc.)* make it a very short-range projectile. The design causes the slug to shed velocity and thus energy at an extremely quick rate, often dropping to subsonic speeds inside of 70 yards.

A cross section of modern full-bore slugs *(left to right)*: Foster slug (as loaded by Winchester, Remington and Federal), Original Brenneke (as loaded by Rottweil), 3-inch Brenneke (as loaded by Rottweil and Brenneke USA), the Cervo slug, and the Italian Gualandi (as loaded by Nitro).

| FOSTER | ORIGINAL BRENNEKE | 3-INCH BRENNEKE | CERVO SLUG | ITALIAN GUALANDI |

the sound barrier effect

Projectiles like shotgun slugs that operate at speeds in the vicinity of the sound barrier face a series of forces that rifle bullets simply fly past. Velocity, you see, has a considerable bearing on the inherent accuracy of a projectile in flight. While increased velocity is generally considered to be good, the most prominent obstacle to slug accuracy is the sonic barrier. At sea level, in dry 65-degree air, the speed of sound is reached at 1,089 feet per second. When General Chuck Yeager, the first pilot to fly faster than the speed of sound, brought his aircraft close to the sound barrier, he suddenly experienced so much buffeting that he had trouble keeping the aircraft flying straight. After passing the barrier his steering ability returned.

The same thing happens to rifled slugs as they slow down into that velocity range. The turbulence created

Prior to the advent of the sabot slug, a shotgun load's effective range was limited by the sound barrier.

As shown in this Winchester laboratory photo, the soft Foster slug *(above left)* is distorted in flight — the "rifling" is often rubbed off by the barrel walls — and thus is very difficult to keep stable when it passes the sonic barrier.

The high-RPM spin of the sabot slug keeps it stable even when it drops below the sonic barrier.

by the sound wave closing behind the slug as its velocity decays to a transonic range actually buffets older-style, less aerodynamic slugs into instability. With Foster-style rifled slugs this commonly occurs at between 63 and 73 yards. If the slug is not perfectly concentric, it will lose its stability. The big difference between the Foster-style slugs of 30 years ago and those of today is a slightly larger diameter and improved production standards that result in more concentric designs. The short effective range was simply an accepted fact and, allowing for a few minor alterations, slug shooting remained virtually the same from the 1930s through the mid-1980s.

Sabot slugs are more resistant to the sonic buffeting due to their stabilizing spin. That's why the advent of rifled barrels *(today every major shotgun manufacturer in the U.S. market offers at least a couple of models)* accelerated slug development at relative warp speed. Rifled barrels first came on the scene in the late 1980s and it soon became apparent that the Brenneke design's high fins were easily destroyed by rifling, making them incompatible with rifled bores. To get a foothold in the new market Brenneke introduced the 600-grain Golden Slug in 1993, just as Ithaca Gun brought out its fast-twist (one turn in 25 inches) 12-gauge Deerslayer II to accommodate the big slug.

enter the "sabot"

The big move came earlier with the development of the saboted slug. "Sabot," pronounced "sah-bow," is a French term for wooden shoes, ranging from the all-wooden shoe of French farmers to the strap-over women's shoes we know as "clogs." Adapting a concept used in artillery ammunition, slug makers started producing smaller diameter, more aerodynamic slugs encased in bore-filling fall-away plastic sleeves called sabots. This allowed the cavernous shotgun bore to throw a much more efficient projectile — and the plastic sleeves grabbed the rifling and imparted a stabilizing spin to the whole unit.

The earliest commercial design came out of California from BRI's (Ballistic Research Industries) Santa Cruz labs, which used a .50-caliber, 1-ounce wasp-waisted pellet with a hollow rear (plugged with a wooden dowel) loaded in a two-piece polyethylene sleeve. The original design of the late 1960s was called the Kelly-McAlvain .50 caliber

Sabot is a French term for the wooden shoes traditionally worn by farmers or strap-over women's shoes. The term is used in artillery ammunition when a bore-filling "shoe" encases a smaller, aerodynamic round. The large bore sabot allows for a larger amount of propellant and the smaller round achieves better velocity and ballistics.

443-grain saboted projectile. Smith & Wesson at one point loaded a later BRI version as police loads (they'd shoot through engine blocks or car and house doors with little deflection) and quickly relabeled them to sell to the hunting market also.

BRI was known for the accuracy potential of its slugs but its products were hampered by a small budget. BRI bought hulls, powders, primers, and other components from whatever vendor had them available at the lowest price. The result was a huge inconsistency in quality and performance from lot to lot. Production was also slow. I'm told that at BRI a production employee actually drilled the rear of each slug and hand-inserted a wooden dowel and sanded it flat before passing the slug on to the loading department. In 1990 Winchester bought the BRI patent and improved it, thanks to its candy store of available powders, wads, hulls and technicians. The next year Federal Cartridge brought out a higher-velocity but visually identical model based on an older BRI patent. The design was very accurate but much too hard to expand effectively in deer-sized game and was markedly slower than full-bore slugs – putting it at a distinct disadvantage for short-range shooting in typical whitetail environments.

The Lightfield Hybred was the first sabot design that expanded effectively when used on deer-sized game.

The sabot's true advantage came farther downrange where the combination of spin and nose-heavy design kept it stable, thereby retaining its energy well past 100 yards, the point where the full-bore slugs had petered out. The tiny Lightfield Ammunition Corporation was formed to produce a design called a Hybred, developed by British designer Tony Kinchin – the first expanding saboted slug. The Lightfield was actually much closer to the 3-inch Brenneke pattern or the similar Activ attached wad design, but encased in a two-piece thin sabot. The Lightfield was a full 547 grains (one ounce and a quarter) of very soft lead with a diameter of .670 inch, which needed little expansion at setback to bring it to bore size. In fact, that's the reason the Hybred design shoots so well out of virtually all rifled barrels. At setback it swells to the diameter of whatever barrel it is in, unlike other sabots.

WINCHESTER   FEDERAL

Both Winchester and Federal produced dimensionally and ballistically identical conventional sabot rounds in the early 1990s. The slugs were very accurate but too hard and too slow to expand when striking deer-sized game.

The Clinton Administration's stringent standards made it virtually impossible for a new company to get authorized for a powder magazine, so Lightfield could not manufacture its own slugs. It contracted Activ Industries in West Virginia to do the original loading, but that work went to Nitrokemia-Fiocchi Ltd. in Hungary when Activ ran into financial hardships in the mid-1990s. Lightfields, in the meantime, have undergone several hull, primer and powder changes but the Hybred slug design has remained fairly constant, even though the originals were swaged and the current versions are cast. The Lightfield Commander series is an entirely different design, which we'll look at later in the chapter.

Winchester bought rights to use the BRI sabot patent and offered its own version in the early 1990s.

Next in the slam-bang development of slugs came Remington's revolutionary Copper Solid – a 1-ounce, .50-caliber slug with an open, slotted nose that was machined out of solid copper bar stock. Machining rather than swaging or casting made the slugs much more consistent and the Copper Solid was a huge lunge forward

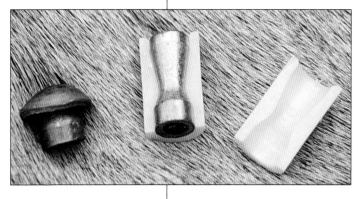

in development in that it was the first rear-weighted slug. It was, in fact, a bullet. The original Copper Solid, while a technological breakthrough, turned out to be a nightmare in application. The unyielding, hard copper stock shot right through things it shouldn't have. "My brother-in-law asked if he could use one of my round bails as a backdrop for a target so he could sight-in his slug gun with Copper Solids," said one Illinois farmer of my acquaintance. "He shot a couple of times at 50 yards and I heard some funny noises. Turns out those damned slugs blew right through the round bails and into my poly water tank on a trailer about 70 yards behind them."

In addition, the hard Copper Solid slugs didn't stretch under pressure in the barrel like softer lead-based slugs, which apparently could cause pressure spikes and damaged barrels. When I noted in a newspaper column that four Ithaca Gun barrels (all from one manufacturing lot) were burst by Copper Solids, I was flooded with similar horror stories of damaged Remington and Mossberg barrels. Hastings' Bob Rott says that he replaced $10,000 worth of his Paradox barrels damaged by Copper Solids and later incurred Big Green's wrath when he began shipping a disclaimer with each new Hastings barrel stating that the warranty was void if the owner used Copper Solids in it. Despite its problems, the Copper Solid design found no legal opposition and the rest of the industry was encouraged to experiment with bullet-style designs.

Early sabot choices offered in the mid-1990s *(left to right)*: Lightfield Hybred, Remington Copper Solid and conventional Federal or Winchester sabot.

young was pioneer

Actually, while history may credit Remington, the true pioneer in the real-bullets-in-sabots area was a tiny Trenton, New Jersey, slug maker named Chris Young. Chris is actually the father of high-velocity sabot slugs in the same way that Karl Foster is the father of the rifled slug. The owner of Gun Servicing, Inc., Young began loading 300-grain, .45-caliber Hornady XTP pistol bullets in cup-like collets of his own design in 1990. In 1995 he began loading a magnum version, using a .50-caliber Barnes X-Bullet – a full year before Federal Cartridge struck a deal with Randy Brooks' bullet company to load a similar round in a sabot of their design. The Federal Barnes EXpander was close enough to the magnum collet so that patents were pulled out and examined very closely. The very malleable but sleekly shaped all-copper Barnes EXpander bullet mushroomed consistently on deer-sized game – something that early sabots simply did not do. It was followed a year later by Remington's "improved" (much softer design) Copper Solid, which was a ballistic and visual carbon copy of the Federal EXpander in a green hull.

The Federal Barnes EXpander and the Improved Remington Copper Solid were virtual ballistic twins.

the high-velocity generation

Meanwhile, Winchester-Olin had been working on a project of its own, using a version of the Partition Gold bullet it had used for pistol and muzzleloader loads, for three years. A product of Winchester's Combined Technologies effort with Nosler, the Partition Gold was a specially jacketed lead core bullet that sat on a partition and was filled with a lead tail in the traditional Nosler Partition design. The bullet was 385 grains compared with the 440-grain norm for conventional sabots (and EXpanders) and had a uniquely high (for slugs) ballistic coefficient of .220. Consider that the average Foster slug's BC is around .060 and the super-accurate Winchester Hi-Impact and Federal Premium sabots were about .101.

Pushing the new slug to high velocity was a problem for Winchester – the faster you drive a load the more muzzle blast turbulence you create. The turbulence surrounds the sabot and bullet in the initial milliseconds of separation *(the sabot petals begin to spread the instant they clear the muzzle)*. In addition, the harder your propellant charge kicks the load at setback (the initial moment at ignition) the more distorted the sabot may become. In fact, Winchester designers found that the higher pressure tended to wrap the sabot around the slug, hampering its release. Finally designers found that by molding an aluminum floor into the plastic sabot for the slug to rest on, the combination would be stiff enough to perform under the higher chamber pressure.

The Winchester Supreme Partition Gold slug burst onto the market with a great deal of hype and was a tremendous retail success, selling out its production runs almost immediately even at a considerably higher retail than any other slug. The new slug showed extraordinary terminal ballistics, extremely flat trajectory at a projected 1,900 fps muzzle velocity and 3,200 foot-pounds of energy at the muzzle. It would have been unique had Hornady not revamped its first failed effort at slug making, the ATP, into the high-velocity H2K Heavy Mag. – a Hornady controlled-expansion bullet loaded to a muzzle velocity of 2,000 feet per second.

High velocity has become the goal of current slug makers when Lightfield introduced the uniquely designed 3- and 3.5-inch Commander series in 2001. The two Commanders project muzzle velocities of 1,800 and 1,900 fps for 500-grain slugs. The Commander's sabot actually remains attached until it penetrates the target, rather than flying off en route. Not only does the design eliminate the ballistic nightmare of shedding the sabot but it also stiffens the load to withstand the increased chamber pressure that comes with higher velocity. The 3.5-inch Commander is the first sabot

The photographs below record the paths, or virtual wound channels, of a Foster slug *(top)*, a Brenneke slug *(center)* and a sabot slug *(bottom)* through a 3-foot block of ballistic gelatin possessing the same mass and density as a deer's body.

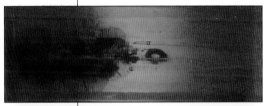
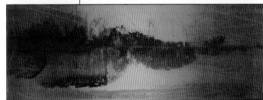
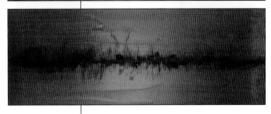

The Hornady XTP (left) and Winchester Partition Gold were among the first lead core, copper jacketed slugs.

of that length and, when it was introduced, had just one rifled-barreled gun chambered to handle it, the Mossberg 835 Ultri-Mag.

Mossberg has since added other models with 3.5-inch chambers and rifled barrels and Remington, Browning, Winchester and Benelli have 3.5-inch guns that can be fitted with rifled barrels, although most of the barrels are only chambered for 3 inches. The 3.5-inch Commander is, in fact, just 30 to 50 fps faster than the 3-inch model with the same slug, attached wad and powder charge. For logistical reasons (shorter free bore) it is probably slightly more accurate than the 3-inch version but the difference in recoil is far less than might be expected. If you've ever shot a 3.5-inch, 12-gauge shotgun for turkeys or geese you know that they kick unmercifully. The additional interior space provided by the half-inch longer hull is an advantage for shotshells but more pellets can be delivered to the pattern. Their 2.25- or 2.5-ounce payloads are the reason for the devastating recoil, but that's not the case in the 3.5-inch Commander slug, which throws only 1 ounce of lead.

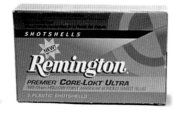

Remington's 12-gauge Core-Lokt Ultra shells contained a 385-grain rifle-bullet type slug *(above left)* in a plastic sabot.

At the same time Brenneke has devised its own high-velocity load, the Super Sabot, which incorporates a sliding copper sleeve over a soft-nosed aluminum projectile. The new load is available in both 2³/4- and 3-inch 12-gauge versions with a top muzzle velocity of 1,640 fps. Brenneke also markets a KO Sabot of similar velocity. This slug is actually the company's 20-gauge smoothbore KO slug encased in a fingered cushion wad that grips the rifling.

In 2003 Brenneke USA introduced the Black Magic slug – a 600-grain, 12-gauge slug for 3-inch chambers. Designed for use in both smooth- and rifled bores, the new black slug has a slightly different rib pattern than the 600-grain Gold Super Magnum and a slightly different power-wad. The CleanSpeed coating, like the Brenneke Gold slug's coating, reduces lead fouling in the barrel and perhaps more importantly, keeps the muzzle and choke tubes completely clean. Its ballistics are identical to the Gold – 1,502 fps muzzle velocity and 3,014 foot-pounds of muzzle energy. In 2003 Dynamit-Nobel, which has been loading Brenneke slugs under the Rottweil label for years, augmented that line with the 12-gauge Rottweil Blitz (2³/4-inch) and Blitz Plus (3-inch) slugs. The Blitz slugs have since been discontinued, but in 2011 Rottweil added the Equal slug for smoothbores, incorporating the big Italian-made Gualandi slug also used by Challenger and others. Rottweil also picked up the design of the Hastings Laser sabot slug after that company went out of business and had it loaded by Polywad (which also loaded the Hastings) as the Laser Plus.

The Brenneke Super Sabot has a unique bullet-like core design with a sliding copper sleeve inside a conventional plastic shotcup sabot.

Remington was busy on the ammunition front with three new shotgun slug designs for 2003. Big Green's new 12-gauge Core-Lokt Ultra slug is a .50-caliber, 385-grain sabot version of its time-honored rifle bullet, encased in a plastic sabot. A 20-gauge, 260-grain version will also be introduced. With a muzzle velocity of 1,900 fps and a better ballistic coefficient (.281) than anything on the market, this one really has promise. Current ballistics rival the Winchester Partition Gold. At the same time Remington is

Fired *(bottom)* and unfired versions of the rock-hard conventional sabot after being fired into ballistic gelatin.

the 3-inch "magnum"

The 3-inch magnum 12-gauge slug has long been a big seller. Americans like muscle and the perceived advantage of these loads made them marketable. "Perceived" is the operative word there. In the early 1990s a noted authority working for an ammunition manufacturing company suggested that I take note of an abnormality in slug shooting the next time I chronographed the various loads on the market. "I think you'll be surprised by the 3-inchers," he said with a wink.

Sure enough, despite the higher velocities and increased energy touted on the packaging and on industry ballistics charts, the 3-inch slugs registered on the chronograph as roughly the same as the 2³/₄-inchers. Sure, there was slightly more recoil but the velocities were very close to those of the supposedly less-powerful slugs — much closer than the manufacturers would have had us believe. "The extra recoil is from the slightly higher pressure caused by a little more ejecta," the slug expert explained when I called him with the findings. The only difference between the 2³/₄-inchers and the 3-inchers is a quarter-inch spacer wad."

It was the same with all of the Foster-style slugs loaded by Winchester, Federal and Remington — the 2³/₄-inch and 3-inch slugs used exactly the same projectile and close to the same amount of powder. The difference was the aforementioned spacer wad. The conventional sabot slugs were the same. The Sporting Arms and Ammunition Manufacturers Institute (SAAMI), which sets specifications for all ammunition and firearms used in the United States, originally limited 12-gauge slugs to 12,500 foot-pounds of chamber pressure and the 2³/₄-inch slugs were loaded to the limit. That left the 3-inchers with no room to advance. Then, in the late 1990s, SAAMI dropped the 12-gauge ceiling to 11,500 foot-pounds but allowed the 3-inchers slightly more.

Finally, in 2001, we saw a 3-inch 12-gauge slug with a different projectile and loading than its 2³/₄-inch counterpart. In fact, the 3-inch Lightfield Commander is a totally different design than the company's 2³/₄-inch Hybred sabot. The Hybred, introduced in 1994, is a 1.25-ounce soft lead projectile with an attached plastic stem wad and a thin two-piece sabot. It is fired at 1,450 feet per second, which is the conventional muzzle velocity of 2³/₄-inch sabot ammunition. The soft Hybred couldn't be pushed faster than 1,500 fps. Any faster and the soft lead would ooze under the pressure, making it difficult to shed the sabot halves efficiently. Thus the Commander design includes a slightly lighter slug encased in a one-piece Delrin sabot that stays attached right into the target. The sabot works like the jacket on a bullet, stiffening the system so that the slug can be driven 1,800 fps. A couple of years later Lightfield stiffened the Hybred design sufficiently to bring out a 3-inch Hybred Elite.

Every manufacturer has a different idea of how long 3 inches is.

Ballistics charts will show 3-inch slugs with more velocity but they are actually very close to the 2³/₄-inch versions.

The difference between 2³/₄-inch and 3-inch Foster slugs is the spacer wad, nothing else.

Lightfield's 2³/₄-Hybred, shown fired and unfired at left, is much softer than the 3-inch Commander (above right).

Top and bottom: The unique full-bore Remington Express BuckHammer and an expanded version of the Remington Express BuckHammer.

The Winchester Platinum Tip slug uses the same reinforced-floor sabot as the Partition Gold.

Remington Core-Lokt Ultra is an example of a state-of-the-art high-velocity, jacketed slug design.

offering a unique, hulking $1^1/_4$-ounce full-bore slug for rifled barrels named the Express BuckHammer. The .73-caliber, 547-grain attached-wad design makes the BuckHammer the highest energy lead shotgun slug available with 2,935 foot-pounds of muzzle energy and 1,600 left at 100 yards. Remington also lit a fuse under its venerable Slugger Foster-style slug design in 2003 with the introduction of the 1,800 fps 12-gauge Slugger High Velocity load. The fastest Foster-style load on the market, the Slugger High Velocity offers 1,517 foot-pounds of energy at the muzzle. Remington achieved these performance plateaus by simply bringing back the 7/8-ounce 12-gauge and 1/2-ounce 20-gauge slug that it shelved in the 1980s and aligned them with updated powder and wads.

Federal introduced a high-velocity version of its Premium Barnes EXpander in 2001, projecting 1,900 fps with a 325-grain Barnes X-Bullet slug *(actually the slug loaded in its 20-gauge EXpander for two years)* in a 12-gauge configuration. In 2002 Winchester came right back with the Platinum Tip sabot slug, an adaptation of the company's FailSafe bullet design – essentially a .50-caliber Black Talon pistol bullet with a silver jacket rather than the brand's customary black. The Platinum Tip is, at 400 grains, slightly heavier and at 1,700 fps, slightly slower than the Partition Gold. It is also slightly less expensive and is specifically designed to perform on deer-sized game. I've found it to be much more forgiving than the Partition Gold in both recoil and in what guns it prefers.

The 20-gauge, 260-grain Winchester Platinum Tip slug came out in 2003, its 1,700 fps muzzle velocity matching that of the 12-gauge version introduced a year earlier. At the same time ,Lightfield came out with a low-velocity, low-recoil $2^3/_4$-inch 12-gauge round called Lightfield Lites, a 1,300 fps round that shoots especially well in rifled choke tubes.

high-velocity slugs' quirks

The newest generation of slugs – the high velocity Winchester Partition Gold, Platinum Tip, DualBond and XP3, Hornady SST, Federal Premium High Velocity Barnes Expander and Tipped Barnes Expander, Federal's Fusion, the Lightfield Commander and Hybred Elite, Remington's Core-Lokt Ultra and Accu-Tip and Brenneke's Super Sabot – will likely sacrifice a little accuracy to achieve hot ballistics. The high-velocity (1,800-2,000 fps) loads operate right on the ragged edge of slug ballistics and are finicky as to which barrels and twist rates they like. Are they necessary for conventional deer hunting? Not really. Are they effective? Well, I killed a 1,850-pound plains buffalo in South Dakota with the Winchester Partition Gold 12-gauge load and my traveling partner Steve Meyer took a bedded Wyoming pronghorn at 191 yards with the same load. Yeah, that's effective.

It will take a truly experienced hand and ideal shooting conditions to notice, but the new high-velocity sabots seem to prefer the faster 1-in-28 inches twist rate *(Marlin, Browning, Winchester, Tar-Hunt, Benelli)* to the 1-34 or 36 twist rates of the others. Lightfield makes the only 16-gauge sabot ammunition as part of its Commander series, and it has just one rifled barrel outlet – the Ithaca M37 Deerslayer and Deerslayer II. There are no 10-gauge or .410 sabot slugs; in fact, only Federal Cartridge even loads rifled slugs for the 10-gauge while all of the big three load half-ounce .410 rifled slugs. Don't expect to ever see sabot slugs in those gauges since, given the infinitesimal fraction of the market that those bores represent, no one is going to start building rifled barrels. No matter how you look at it, slug shooting has come a long way and it doesn't look like that evolution will end anytime soon.

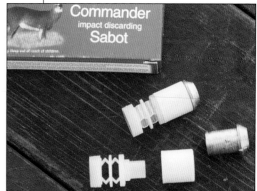

The Lightfield Commander is the only 16-gauge sabot slug on the market.

"other" brands of slugs

The major manufacturers, Winchester, Remington, Federal, Brenneke and Lightfield, should be credited with leading the astounding leap forward that slug shooting has experienced in the last 25 years. There are other options, such as Fiocchi USA, Dynamit-Nobel, Kent and PMC slugs as well as the Canadian-built Challenger, which are North American companies loading Italian and German slugs. The familiar all-plastic hulled Activ design is now loaded in Spain, and other nations weigh in with the Czech-built Sellier & Bellot slug, the French Sauvestre Ball Fleche and the Latvian-made Ddupleks slugs. But they and others are hard-pressed to find shelf space among the totally adequate array of big-name domestic loads.

Despite this remarkable choice of relatively new high-performance slugs available to the American shotgunner, there are still an appreciable number of shooters who won't ever be satisfied with the status quo. Maybe they're caught up in the excitement of the expanding technology. Maybe they see a chance for windfall profits by moving faster than the major manufacturers. Whatever the reason, every year several folks send me samples of their home-built "innovations." They usually consist of a hand cast projectile of offbeat configuration that the designers feel is going to make them millionaires and instantly render all other slugs obsolete. Most have some glaring problem that is evident during the first session at the range, but sometimes a bizarre design does work.

For example, I remember when shooters smirked at the idea of putting a plastic sleeve on a .50-caliber hourglass pellet and shooting it through a rifle bore. But the sabot design survived the scoffs and eventually put originator Bob Sowash right up there with Karl Foster and Wilhelm Brenneke as historic figures in slug shooting. Historic names? How about Chris Young or Ray Filogomo? Young, a New Jersey gunsmith and custom handloader, was mentioned earlier as the first to design a sabot shot-

Nitro loads the Gualandi slug in both 3-inch and 3.5-inch loads.

gun load around a large-bore, controlled expansion pistol bullet before Federal Cartridge and Barnes Bullets got together; before Winchester-Nosler's Combined Technologies, before Hornady, etc. You've undoubtedly read that Lightfield's Commander was the first $3^1/_2$-inch 12-gauge slug when it was introduced in 2001. Nope, Filogomo's tiny upstate New York shop was producing $3^1/_2$-inchers loaded with Gualandi slugs in the early 1990s under the Nitro Company label.

Chris Young was a dedicated slug hunter who was excited by the introduction of rifled barrels and saboted slugs for shotguns but found himself disappointed by the design's lack of expansion and "punch" in deer hunting situations. He also recoiled at having to pay $1.50 per round. His original collet cup design featured a 300-grain, .45-caliber Hornady XTP pistol bullet as the projectile with a thick-walled one-piece collet sabot housing. "Our standard slug (1,450 fps) works best in $2^3/_4$-inch chambers and barrels with 1-in-34-to-36 twist but is a little light in some autoloaders," says Young, who has run a gunsmithing shop in Trenton for nearly 30 years. "Our magnum (1,500 fps) seems to like $2^3/_4$- or 3-inch chambers and shoots very well in some of the faster-twist barrels like the 1-in-28 Tar-Hunt rifle."

Young also loaded the .45 Hornady XTP in $2^3/_4$- and 3-inch 20-gauge loads as well as the smaller but faster 250-grain .45 Hornady. He finds outstanding accuracy in 20-gauge guns with fast (1-in-24) rifling. In the mid-1990s, years before Federal started loading Barnes' .50-caliber all-copper EXpander bullet, Young began loading a big Barnes bullet in his collet sabot and calling it a Magnum Collet Cup. In fact, Federal had to find a way around Young's patent in order to build the Federal Barnes EXpander.

Chris Young's Collet Cup slug was the first bullet-in-a-sleeve design.

Filogomo, who moved his Nitro Company shop from Gilboa, New York, to Mountain Grove, Missouri, in 2002, has been producing specialty slug, buckshot, waterfowl, turkey and defense loads since the early 1990s. Nitro uses Fiocchi hulls and loads moly-coated Italian-built 12- and 20-gauge Gualandi slugs that provide remarkable accuracy out of rifled or smoothbore barrels. Nitro's 20-gauge Gualandis are $7/_8$ ounce with a muzzle velocity of 1,420-1,440 feet per second in $2^3/_4$- and 3-inch hulls. The 12s are $^{11}/_8$-ounce slugs launched at 1,600 fps in the 3-inch version and 1,650 fps in the unique $3^1/_2$-incher. Even more interesting is the "200-yard Accuracy Slug" that Filogomo loads in 12- and 10- gauge for smoothbore guns. "I actually get more accuracy out of a smoothbore than a rifled bore," Ray says. His 200-yarder is either a Teflon-coated 1- or 11/8-ounce .60-caliber round ball, or an AG Slug *(lead ball with an attached plastic platform)* fired at 1,570 to 1,700 fps, depending on the gauge, that is capable of a 4-inch group and 4-inch drop at 200 yards. He also builds a 1,560 fps, 150-yard "Accuracy Load" for certain rifled barrels based on the moly-coated 490-grain Gualandi slug.

Challenger loads the Gualandi slug in its Canadian-made shells.

correct handling of slugs

I could hardly believe the printout from the Oehler 35P chronograph. Right there in the bright June sunlight it read that two of the four slug brands I was timing were nearly 400 feet per second slower than factory specs. I'd taken the slugs directly from storage in my shop to the range. What was the matter with them? Were they duds, inadvertently underloaded, or was the chronograph working poorly? After running a check on the chronograph parameters and the other two brands of slugs that I was shooting (which came directly from the factory), there was no doubt that the original two brands were slow – very slow. Granted, the velocities that the manufacturers list are derived from 30-inch, air-gauged pressure barrels fired from machines in climate-controlled, windless tunnels, but the difference in barrel length and type didn't explain 400 feet per second.

Remington's High Velocity Slugger is the fastest Foster design on the market.

"When they are around moisture, remember that slugs have a hole in the roof," explained Tar-Hunt custom slug gun builder Randy Fritz, who also serves as director of load development with Lightfield Ammunition. "Moisture slips around that slug and sabot very easily and compromises the powder." Randy is a good friend of mine and you'll find him mentioned throughout this book since he's the preeminent mind in slug shooting today. He also cringes at the way I do things. The guy is a national-caliber benchrest shooter. He's the type of guy who weighs cases and bullets to the nearest grain; he is used to glass-slick actions with tolerances so tight a couple of grains of sand will jam it. If his 5-shot 100-yard benchrest rifle groups "swell" to a quarter-inch, it's time to scrap that barrel. Suffice it to say, I'm not like that. My shop at the time was unheated and a tad drafty. The slugs had been stored there for a few months during the winter and spring. The other slugs that had chronographed as expected had arrived only a couple of days prior to the shoot and had been stored in my office.

Temperature and moisture have profound effects on slug performance – a lot more than I realized. Not only do atmospheric conditions affect powder but plastic hulls (roll crimps) and sabots (dimensions) also change with temperature and humidity. The garage, wood shed, barn, etc., are definitely not the places to store slugs. Even if they've been stored correctly in a sealed container, if you open it and leave them in the trunk of your car for a few days, the ballistic characteristics are bound to change. But if you have a batch of slugs that gets fouled, don't throw them out or give them to your no-account brother-in-law. Fritz says that taking them into a climate-controlled setting (your house should do) for a few weeks will likely dry them out enough to perform well again. Keeping them in the house during the winter, where the temperature is relatively constant and the humidity is low, is the ideal.

Kevin Howard of Missouri took this mule deer at 165 yards with a Winchester Partition Gold slug and a Browning Gold shotgun.

But what do you do when the humidity of spring and summer hit? "After they are dried out, I'd suggest packing them in air-tight covers – Zip-Loc bags are fine – and storing them in a cheap cooler with a tight lid," says Fritz. "I keep them in that kind of storage year-around, and don't forget to maintain that kind of situation in hunting season, too. If you're carrying them in your pocket, or a pack, or — worse yet — one of those bands on the stock, they're absorbing moisture," says Fritz. "If you get wet, it's just common sense that they're wet, too." Granted, if you're only shooting 40-50 yards at a buck, the difference in performance isn't likely to be noticeable. But there will be a difference, nevertheless. The temperature-humidity phenomenon affects performance in all ammunition. Military specs call for ammunition to be "calmed" by 1,000 pounds of chamber pressure before being issued.

"If you develop a hunting load for your rifle in Alaska, don't come back home and shoot it," Fritz says, referring to the effect temperature has on chamber pressure. "People who live in the South and Southwest carry their ammo to the range in coolers to keep it from 'cooking.' " The aforementioned phenomenon is more pronounced with slugs, however. If your slugs lose or gain 300 feet per second in velocity, it translates to thousands of pounds in chamber pressure. A shift of 2,000-3,000 pounds in a rifle, where chamber pressure is 50,000-60,000 foot-pounds, is inconsequential. But a shift of that size in a shotgun chamber, where pressure is usually less than 12,000 foot-pounds, the percentage of loss is significant and can translate to several inches difference in elevation 100 yards downrange.

Slugs are loaded under controlled conditions of extremely low humidity and high temperature — making them "hot" ballistically. The reasoning is that the slugs will take on moisture during shipping and storage and velocity will fall into the specified range. "If you sight-in your slug gun in July or August, don't expect it to shoot to the same zero in hunting season," Fritz advises. "If you don't believe me, sight-in a few slugs on a summer day and put the rest of the box in the freezer. The next day take those slugs and see where they print in relation to the previous day's batch." To a guy like Randy, whose definition of accuracy differs profoundly from yours and mine, this is a troublesome world. "You know," said the man I consider the most knowledgeable on slugs and slug guns in the world, "if you spend enough time around this stuff, you start to wonder how we ever hit anything at all."

The Federal Barnes EXpander uses a heavy-walled plastic sabot.

other specialty loaders

Magnum Performance Ballistics (Polywad) of Macon, Georgia, loads a unique frangible 2³/₄-inch 12-gauge Quik-Shok sabot slug that gathers 1,500 feet per second at the muzzle and splits into three distinct 160-grain sections upon penetration of the target — sort of like reverse buckshot. The projectile is actually an imitation of the Foster-style slug without the rifling groves. It is 0.68 inch in diameter as opposed to the .50-caliber sizings of most sabots other than Lightfield. The 492-grain (1¹/₈ ounces) Quik-Shok slug reliably segments after penetrating liquid or tissue,

Polywad's frangible Quik-Shok sabot slug (below) fragments upon impact into three segments that disperse in a 6-inch circle providing some of the effect of a load of #00 buckshot (right).

even at ranges beyond 100 yards. Loader Jay Menefee notes that when the slug is fired into 10 percent ballistic gelatin, the three segments penetrate 13-15 inches and provide a "circle of dispersion" of at least 6 inches. So why would anyone want a frangible slug? Well, for one thing, like any frangible projectile, the design eliminates ricochets and/or deflections. If the slug misses the animal it will expand to a large, ellipsoidal shape when impacting a hard surface. This drastically reduces velocity and energy and limits its post-impact range.

"But the real plus for hunters is the rapid energy transfer diffused over a large area within the target," says Menefee. "The dispersion action of the segments creates massive hemorrhaging." Each of the three segments "promotes compression of nerve-laden tissues which become trapped between expanding temporary cavities, resulting in maximum motor interruption," according to the Polywad hype. "The segmentation also increases the probability of striking or affecting one or more vital organs, even if the shot is poorly placed," Menefee says. The pure lead Quik-Shok slug is contained within a collapsible, 4-petal polymer cup that falls away upon exiting the muzzle. A nylon pusher disk acts as a buffer between it and the base of the slug. Upon firing, the slug expands radially inside the polymer cup. Like the Lightfield Hybred, the Quik-Shok is final-swaged in the bore, providing custom-fit, regardless of barrel dimensions.

Unlike solid, hourglass-type sabots, the collapsible cup tempers recoil by modifying the impulse curve. This results in a milder perceived recoil. In fact, Menefee claims that the Quik-Shok sabot slug recoils less than any other 12-gauge slug on the market and that the wad (like other sabots) also eliminates barrel leading. Although 100-yard accuracy was poor and penetration drops dramatically with frangible ammunition as they slow, I was able to consistently group the Quik-Shoks at around $1^1/_4$ to $1^1/_2$ inches at 50 and 75 yards.

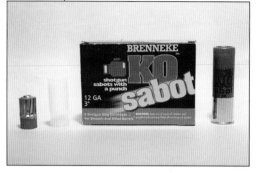

Both the high-velocity Brenneke KO sabot load (above top) and the Polywad Quik-Shok round (above) use a plastic or nylon buffer disk between the projectile and the sabot cup.

hevi-shot:
a new generation?

Polywad also loads EnvironMetal's new Hevi-Shot slug. The 1-ounce, .68-caliber, tungsten-nickel, Foster-shaped cup is visually similar to the Polywad's Quik-Shok. In fact, the opaque Fiocchi hulls and the cushion wads are identical. The Hevi-Shot slug has a slightly thicker orange pusher disk to fill the hull space left by its shorter length. The Hevi-Shot slug was a work in progress when I tested it in 2002, getting 2- to 3-inch three-shot accuracy at 50 yards with a rifled bore and 5- to 6-inch groups at the same distance when fired through a smoothbore. The Hevi-Shot slug is much harder than the Quik-Shok, however, and the bore fit was critical since it didn't deform at setback to conform to the chamber and barrel like its Polywad cousin. EnvironMetal tried other slug configurations to no avail and continues to work on designs that should eventually be accurate enough to take advantage of the tungsten alloy's higher velocities and devastating penetration.

foreign brands

The American branch of the Italian Fiocchi company, Rottweil's Equal slug, Nitro and the Quebec-based Challenger company also load Gualandi slugs in their 12-gauge hulls. Sellier & Bellot of the Czech Republic loads its own Brenneke-style attached wad slug that is visually similar to the Italian-made Cervo slug formerly loaded by Fiocchi and Activ. Activ's current slug and unique all-plastic (no brass cap) hull are its own design. One of the most bizarre examples of foreign munitions work is French-made Sauvestre Ball Fleche – a 12-gauge saboted "dart" for wont of a better description. They are not to be confused with the "flechette" loads made by Remington and others for military use.

The American flechette consists of a shotgun hull full of razor-sharp tungsten slivers. That load is remarkably accurate even at extreme range (300 yards) and its lack of weight and energy is more than offset by its hideous tissue-rending potential. Unlike the American flechette, the Sauvestre Ball Fleche flechette is a single projectile encased in a two-piece plastic sabot sleeve. The unique projectile looks like a miniature SAM missile, complete with a plastic finned stabilizing tail. It's billed at 1,900 fps in its 3-inch, 12-gauge design but while it didn't achieve quite that in my 25-inch test barrel, the 1,750 fps average that it did post was impressive. The $2^{3}/_{4}$-inch version was about 150 fps slower but quite accurate at 50-60 yards. The slug comes apart quite readily when it hits something and I've yet to summon sufficient nerve to try it on deer. The 396-grain weight and dainty design just don't make it look like a game-getter but I've known some hunters (both smoothbore and rifled barrel users) who claim great success with it.

The Sauvestre Ball Fleche was distributed for a time on these shores, but I haven't seen them here in years. While I've never seen the Aquila brand slugs in this country, they are regionally available through Centurion Ordnance in Texas and the projectiles themselves are available for handloading through Ballistic Products Inc. The Northern Mexican company makes a unique $1^{3}/_{4}$-inch 12-gauge slug featuring a $^{7}/_{8}$-ounce slug launched at 1,252 fps and a similarly unique 8-gauge industrial slug load that lists an unbelievable 3-ounce payload and a muzzle velocity of 1,575 fps. Winchester also markets an 8-gauge industrial slug. That unique payload is fired from table-mounted guns to knock chinks off the inside

The unique Sauvestre Ball Fleche (shown above with and without the ribbed sabot) is a fin-stabilized projectile contained in a two-piece ribbed plastic sabot. *(below)*.

walls of kilns and silos. They are not aerodynamic and lack the expansion characteristics of sporting slugs.

the 20-gauge comes of age

I am a convert. For a long time I've looked at the 20-gauge slug as a watered-down version of what a deer load should be – namely 12-gauge. Oh, it's not that the smaller bore didn't have its place. The reduced recoil and lighter guns were fine if you needed or sought such things and were willing to limit your shots. I've known plenty of women, kids and small-framed men for whom the 20-gauge is ideal. There are more than a few experienced still-hunters whose ability I admire who prefer the challenge involved in using the 20, but I've never been into limiting myself in the deer woods. Regulations already do that. So I use the most efficient equipment that I can under the rules. Personally translated, that means 12-gauge ordnance.

Ballisticians much smarter than I have long been of the opinion that the 20's tighter bore and more streamlined projectile holds more ballistic potential than the bulky 12. But the theory was that the only way for the smaller bore to achieve its potential was to load a 1-ounce slug in a 3-inch hull. Do that, however, and you've eliminated the reduced recoil that gives the 20 its allure. Besides, I'm told that the 20 represents only about 10 percent of the retail slug market. Nobody is going to do much research and development to feed that little niche. Any advances in the 20-gauge are simply through technology that drips down from 12-gauge development.

All of this explains why I was so skeptical when Winchester said we were going to hunt pigs with the new Winchester Partition Gold 20-gauge sabot at the Tejon Ranch. Wild hogs, you see, are grizzled, thick-hided, extremely sturdy and stubborn beasts with ugly dispositions when they are crossed. On a previous hunt at the same famed southern California ranch I'd found that the hogs are very difficult to put down, even with quality rifle ammo like Federal's 180-grain Trophy Bonded .30-06. Now I consider the Trophy Bonded, designed by the late Jack Carter but now exclusively in the capable hands of the Federal Cartridge Company, to be one of the

The author poses with a 140 B & C buck taken while hunting in Arkansas with Winchester Platinum Tip 20-gauge slugs and a Browning Gold 20 autoloader.

most effective hunting bullets ever devised. Despite this, a couple of those well-hit Tejon boars retained sufficient spunk to take a tusk-snapping run at me before a finishing shot put an end to their feistiness.

One can imagine my mindset, therefore, when going afield after the same prey, in the same venue, with a small bore shotgun. Suffice it to say, however, as I did in the opening paragraph, that I am now a convert. Using the Winchester 20-gauge Partition Gold and Winchester 1300 Deer Special pump guns (1-in-24 rifling twist), eight of us took pigs ranging upward of 400 pounds — a couple of them at more than 120 yards — in the four-day sojourn in southern California. It was, to say the least, an impressive showing. Any slug that'll dump those rock-ribbed, determined beasts is more than sufficient for any whitetail, anywhere, under any conditions. In subsequent range testing using bull-barreled H&R 925, a Tar-Hunt Mountaineer and a Remington 870 with a Hastings Paradox barrel, the new Winchester Partition load consistently showed muzzle velocities between 1,830 and 1,900 feet per second, single-hole groups at 50 yards and some real zingers at 100.

The modern 20-gauge offers lighter recoil but, in some instances, the same ballistics as 12-gauge guns and loads.

Two years later I took the first-ever deer felled by the Winchester Platinum Tip 20-gauge slug, two mature does — one at 113 yards — at Wingmead Estate in Arkansas. I dropped a couple more does at home with 100-plus yard shots and my hairy-chested bias against the 20-gauge was gone forever. No, the 20-gauge is no longer the red-haired stepchild of the slug gun market. The Winchester loads which retains more velocity at 125 yards than other 20-gauge slugs boast at the muzzle, still packs nearly a half-ton of energy at 200 yards. Performance like that outstrips all but the best high-velocity 12-gauge slug loads and approximates (on paper) that of some old centerfire rifle loads. True, the experts' fondness for a full-ounce slug in the 20 hasn't been realized. There are still a few pipsqueak 20-gauge slug loads out there, but, in addition to the high-velocity Winchesters (PartitionGold, Platinum tip, DualBond), I've been impressed with the performance of the 3-inch Federal Barnes Tipped Expanders and Lightfield's hulking 385-grain Hybred Mag-20 in saboted loads and the 3-inch Brenneke in smoothbore guns. Most of the 20-gauge Foster and some of the other 20-gauge sabots, however, should be limited to 75-yard effective ranges. Check the ballistic tables for the distance where a slug drops below 900 foot-pounds of energy. Beyond that range its penetration on deer-sized game will become questionable.

the 16-gauge makes a comeback

No less an authority than the legendary Jack O'Connor once voiced the opinion that the 16-gauge was probably the ideal bore size for shotgun slugs. That opinion was offered back when slug shooting was pretty crude, well before the advent of high-tech sabot slugs and rifled barrels. Back then every shotgun manufacturer included 16-gauges in their product line. O'Connor felt the bore diameter and its relation to the powder charge gave better ballistics than either the 20- or 12-gauge guns with more efficiency and was typically more accurate.

The Lightfield Commander 16 is designed for rifled barrels but also shoots well out of certain smoothbore 16s.

Unfortunately, the 16-gauge was phased out of production by most companies in the early 1970s because the lightweight, soft-recoiling 20 offered everything that the powerful 12 didn't and vice versa. There was no need for a middle-bore gun. Randy Fritz, who helps develop loads for Lightfield Ammunition, agreed with O'Connor's assessment of the 16. Well known as a proponent of wildcat loads on the benchrest rifle circuit, Fritz ventured into uncharted waters when he brought out the company's 16-gauge Commander slug in 2000.

The Commander was the industry's first 16-gauge sabot slug. Since sabot slugs are designed for rifled barrels and no one in the industry was building a rifled barrel gun in that bore, the decision might have seemed a bit silly. But Fritz had secretly been working with Ithaca Gun on the development of just such a gun to co-launch the 21st century 16-gauge. Ithaca — which wisely caters to the historic appeal shown by Baby Boomers — became the only American company to produce a 16-gauge gun in more than 25 years when it went back into production with a 16-gauge version of its Model 37 Featherlight pump in 1998. It sold out its first couple of production runs.

Ithaca once went nose to nose with industry giants like Remington and Winchester as a major firearms manufacturer but like many gun companies, the venerable company struggled through the 1980s and was forced to downsize. Since that time the small central New York-based company has sought to fill niches in the shotgun market. Thus, it came as no surprise when Ithaca teamed with similarly small Lightfield to produce a rifled barrel version of the 16-gauge Model 37. The Commander develops 1,650 feet per second at the muzzle with a projectile that's just a hair under an ounce — a combination that makes its energy compare favorably with conventional 12-gauge slugs.

A hunter takes aim with an Ithaca 16-gauge Deerslayer slug gun. When loaded with the Lightfield Commander round, the Ithaca develops nearly as much muzzle energy as a 12-gauge.

Buckshot

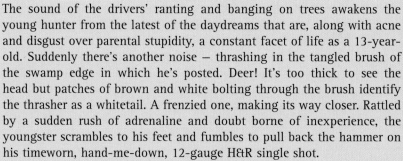

what about buckshot?

The sound of the drivers' ranting and banging on trees awakens the young hunter from the latest of the daydreams that are, along with acne and disgust over parental stupidity, a constant facet of life as a 13-year-old. Suddenly there's another noise — thrashing in the tangled brush of the swamp edge in which he's posted. Deer! It's too thick to see the head but patches of brown and white bolting through the brush identify the thrasher as a whitetail. A frenzied one, making its way closer. Rattled by a sudden rush of adrenaline and doubt borne of inexperience, the youngster scrambles to his feet and fumbles to pull back the hammer on his timeworn, hand-me-down, 12-gauge H&R single shot.

The young buck had been bedded in the gnarled thicket; content to lie in the cool shadows where it had sought solace from roving farm dogs and the strange noises and scents that had become so strong in recent days. Driven from its bed by the sounds of the approaching drivers, the 6-pointer's pell-mell dash down an escape route is interrupted by the sudden appearance of the bumbling Woolrich-clad figure. Just as the buck veers off the trail to avoid contact, the youngster rams the gunstock to his shoulder and, unmindful of the barrel's front bead, fires a load of "double-aught" buckshot toward the now-broadside buck just 20 yards away. The buck instantly slams nose-first into the brush and thrashes away the final seconds of its life. Then it's still. Over the ringing in his ears the youngster hears the drivers, their raucous passage not yet completed. None realize that one of their teen-aged counterparts has just joined the exclusive ranks of successful deer hunters — a scenario that will be played and replayed in his mind so long as it functions in this life.

The 2-year-old buck, its heart and lung area smashed by 10 of the load's 12 pellets, is virtually bled out by the time the boy's dad approaches the stand 10 minutes after the shot. "Did you shoot?" Dad asks, ducking through the brush. "Yeah," said the youngster, his feigned calmness crumbling by the second. Then, "Oh Dad, it's a buck. I got a buck!" The man steps through the forest understory, looks at the young buck and puts his arm around the awestruck, trembling youngster. An abiding sense of pride of something shared and a task completed fills both. The father kneels down, runs a forefinger over one of the pellet holes in the

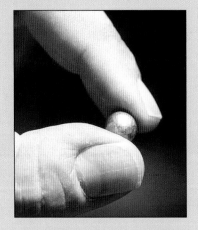

Buckshot pellets can pierce human skin at about 400 yards but the effective range of a full pattern is only 40 yards.

Next page:
Copper-plated buckshot, buffered with grex, is the modern state-of-the-art form of the traditional deer load.

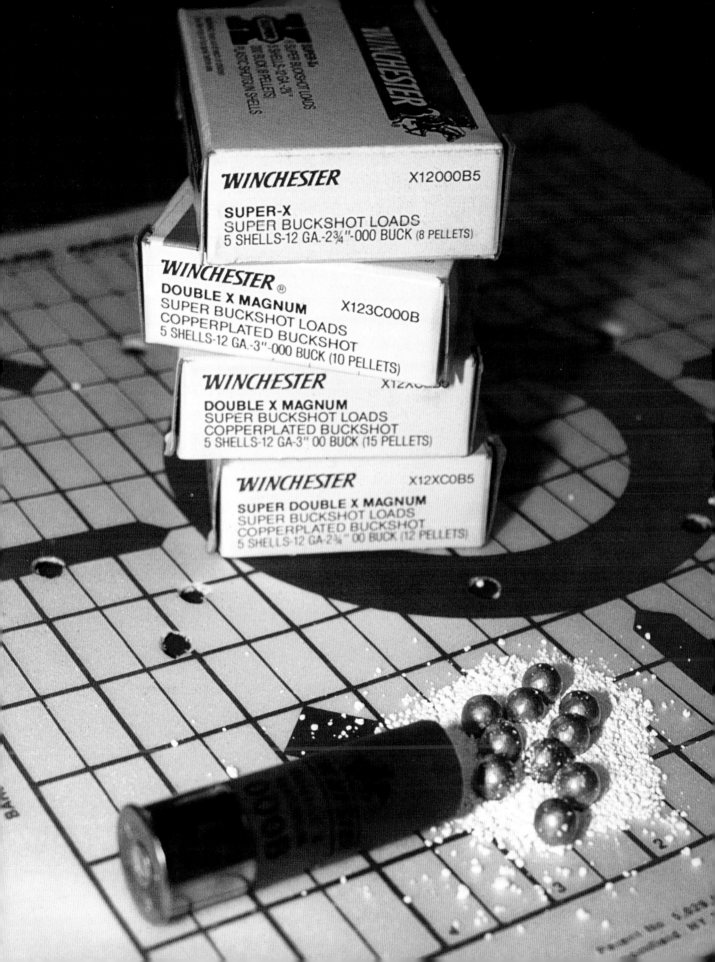

buck's chest and dabs the bloody finger on his beaming son's nose. "Now the work begins, deer hunter," says the dad, unsheathing his knife. The scene has been played out thousands of times from the swamps of the Southeast and Atlantic Seaboard's coastal lowlands to the suburban hardwoods of the Northeast and eastern Midwest.

Buckshot is a time-honored and effective load for deer. That is, it's effective provided you understand and operate within its limits. There would be no argument from old-time tiger hunters of India and Nepal, guides tracking wounded lions or bears, or those combat Marines that found a Remington, Ithaca, Winchester, Mossberg or Browning pump gun loaded with No. 00 buck a comforting companion in the decidedly inhospitable environs of Southeast Asia. Yes, buckshot can be very effective, but that effectiveness is based on the cumulative effect of the entire pattern and with most loads and guns beyond 30-40 yards that pattern deteriorates to the point that you're relying far more on a lucky hit than ballistics. In fact, U.S. Army specs note 40 yards as the absolute effective range for 00 buck used on humans. The same could be said for 00 as a deer load in most contexts. There is an exception *(Hevi-Shot)*, which we'll examine later in this chapter.

Buckshot's effective range is far less than its lethal range, however. Large buckshot pellets' size and retained energy make them lethal out to 300 yards under the right conditions and can easily pierce human flesh at more than 400. So much for the idea that it is "safe" in deer-drive situations. Any slug, full-bore or sabot, 20- or 12-gauge, has a much, much more extensive effective range than buckshot and, although the margin for error is slightly less, is every bit as deadly in close quarters. That being said, I've got a friend in Virginia, where shotguns are mandated for deer hunting in some counties, who will not use slugs. Everyone he knows and hunts with opts for buckshot. "Oh slugs are just too powerful," he says. "They shoot too far." To each his own, as they say.

facts about buckshot

Buckshot has been a popular and effective load since blackpowder days and is still the load mandated for deer hunting in specific areas of at least 10 states. It's legal in 29 states, although five of them don't have any whitetails. Like all shotgun loads, buckshot has improved markedly in the last couple of decades. Development of the shotcup, copper plating, improved lead-antimony or tungsten *(Hevi-Shot)* mixes and granulated plastic buffering have turned the once willy-nilly patterning characteristics of buckshot into an even more devastating tool.

At one time, users of No. 00 *(double-aught)* buckshot found patterns extremely ragged at close range – to the point where a deer-sized target might be missed altogether at 40 yards. Like any shotgun scatter load, the problem is that the bigger the pellet *(00 pellets are .33 caliber; 000 are .36)*, the less room it has to negotiate in the crowded confines of a shotgun bore. I've long heard — and, admittedly, believed without checking — that backbored barrels gave demonstrably better patterning perform-ance than conventional diameter barrels. That may have been true in the old days when the majority of the soft, unplated pellets were damaged or worn by the barrel walls as they sorted themselves out en route to the muzzle. More recent patterning sessions, however, with plated or harder pellets showed me that maybe backboring wasn't the right direction for buckshot shooters.

"I analyze paper *(patterns)* all the time and I've found that backboring or lengthening forcing cones actually hurts buckshot and turkey load patterns," says Ray Filogomo, owner of Nitro Company Ammunition and one of the best shotgun minds I know. "The more you open that bore the more finicky the gun gets. It [backboring or cone lengthening] works well for steel shot and waterfowl loads — it gives you that nice round, even pattern but it tends to open the core. And core density is what you're looking for in buckshot or turkey loads." Ray suggests instead finding the correct diameter choke tube *(he deals exclusively with Joe Morales' Rhino Choke Tubes in Florida).* For 12-gauge guns shooting 00 buck he suggests a tight .665 or .655 choke constriction, depending on the gun; 10-gauge chokes should be .690. Nitro coats many of its buckshot loads in a PTFE (Teflon) derivative to protect barrels and has also added a Hevi-Shot buckshot load.

Interestingly, Remington introduced a 12-gauge Hevi-Shot buckshot load in 2003 to join those produced by Hevi-Shot parent company, Environ-Metal, which are loaded by Polywad out of Georgia. Hevi-Shot is a proprietary tungsten-nickel mix that was actually developed by metallurgist Darryl Amick in his Sweet Home, Oregon, garage, then marketed to the various big munitions companies. All passed at first, which convinced Amick to start EnvironMetal and Polywad began loading for waterfowl, turkey and upland bird loads for him. When Winchester parted ways with Bismuth shortly after the turn of the century, it took another look at Hevi-Shot but balked at the pricing.

Hevi-Shot is actually denser than lead and harder. It's become a revolutionary turkey and waterfowl load but I think that its most effective application may well be in buckshot. Unlike lead pellets, which are generally drop-formed, Hevi-Shot buckshot pellets are powdered metal pressed into a spherical shape and impregnated with resin to give them cohesiveness. Hevi-Shot's extreme density and remarkable patterning

BUCKSHOT SIZE
Buckshot (in inches):

000 buck	0.360 inch
00 buck	0.330 inch
0 buck	0.320 inch
No. 1 buckshot	0.300 inch
No. 2 buckshot	0.270 inch
No. 3 buckshot	0.250 inch
No. 4 buckshot	0.240 inch

* Photograph enlarged

Hevi-Shot buckshot offers more pene-tration and farther effective range than conventional lead buckshot loads.

capabilities extend the effective range of buckshot into heretofore uncharted territory. Simply put, it patterned tighter at much longer ranges and carried its energy much, much farther than anything I've ever shot.

Filogomo concurs, "Hevi-Shot is remarkable stuff. The pellets aren't even round which we always thought was a prerequisite of good patterning. The density, a factor that we never factored in before, makes the pellets, regardless of shape, fly straight." I am among those who agree with Ray's assessment. "Remarkable stuff is right," says Jay Menefee of Polywad. "You can drop this stuff on your concrete garage floor and the pellets will break like china. Yet they are so hard they'll shoot through an animal without deforming." Not everyone wants that "blow-through" effect, however. Many veteran buckshot users resist the hard stuff, including copper-plated buckshot, for that very reason – they want the pellets to deform and dump their energy into the animal instead of using it to blow exit holes.

patterning buckshot

Because patterning conventional buckshot is often seen as difficult, many buckshot hunters opted for smaller shot such as No. 4 *(.24 caliber)*, which patterned much denser than the larger shot. The lethality of No. 4 shot, however, is questionable beyond 20-30 yards. If you talked to old-time buckshot hunters, full choke was the only logical choice. But with today's improved choke systems, and with the plastic sleeves and buffer keeping the shot from being deformed in the barrel, good patterns can be obtained with modified or even improved cylinder choking. New loads, including the relatively new Number 000 *(.36 caliber pellets)*, are more effective

The effective range of various buckshot loads is determined by how well it patterns out of your gun and choke.

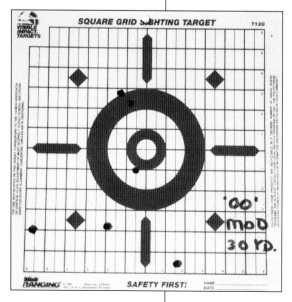
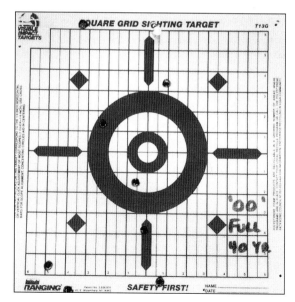

than ever in open-choke guns, too.

With today's loads, effective patterning ranges have lengthened appreciably. For instance, Number 00 plated lead today, fired through a full-choke 12-gauge barrel, would probably average 50 percent *(six of 12 pellets)* in the traditional patterning target of a 30-inch circle at 70 yards. Just 20 years ago a 50 percent pattern could be achieved at no longer than 40 yards. In testing for this book, however, I regularly achieved 100 percent patterns less than 20 inches in diameter at 40 yards with 00 Hevi-Shot fired through a .665 choke tube in a 25-inch Ithaca barrel. But please note that I'm talking about "effective patterning ranges." This is not an endorsement of or suggestion that one take 70-yard shots with buckshot, although the effective range is appreciably longer with Hevi-Shot. Back to patterning, while a 30-inch pattern is a fine criterion for wing shooting birds, we're aiming at the 12- to 16-inch vital area in a deer that can fit its cardio-pulmonary system inside a basketball.

This being the case, a 10-inch pie plate is a realistic buckshot target. A couple of years ago I took to the range with a Browning Auto-5 and Ithaca Model 87, both with interchangeable but different make choke tubes and a box full of Winchester and Brenneke $2^3/4$- and 3-inch Number 00 and Number 000 buckshot loads. In an extended testing session with both guns it was clear that the Number 00 buck wouldn't reliably put more than eight of its pellets in a pie plate-sized target at 30 yards. With some choke constrictions I didn't even get four pellets in the target. Some loads liked full choke, others improved cylinder and I found that just a tiny change in constriction could make a dramatic difference in pattern density.

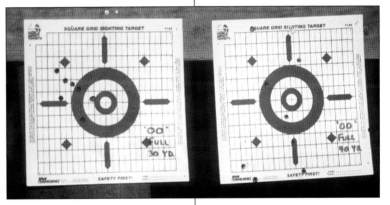

Top: Comparison of 00 buckshot patterns with Modified choke *(left)* and Full choke *(center & right)* at 30 yards.

Bottom: Full choke patterns fired at 30 *(left)* and 40 *(right)* yards.

choke considerations

Interior barrel diameters make a big difference in patterning as well as choke choice. All shotgun bores – particularly older ones – vary slightly in internal diameter, which is why a choke tube will pattern differently when screwed into different barrels. The degree of choke in a barrel is simply a measure of constriction from the bore to the muzzle. Since interior barrel dimensions often vary by as much as 10-15 thousandths of an inch, gun to gun, there is a better way of determining your choke. The true choke size is determined by the difference between the diameter of the bore relative to the diameter of the constriction. By subtracting the diameter of the choke from that of the bore you will be able to determine the amount of constriction (choke) you have regardless of the roll-stamp on the barrel. That measurement is what really counts. That's why the same load may pattern differently in your gun than in your buddy's, even if you use the same choke tube.

Comparison of 000 buckshot patterns with modified choke *(above left)* and full choke *(above right)* at 30 yards.

For instance, if you have a choke tube that is "improved cylinder" relative to the 0.719 bore of a Beretta Urika 391, the same choke tube will be "modified" if used in a barrel of 0.742, which is the size of a backbored Browning Gold. But if your barrel's interior diameter measures 0.732 that same choke tube would represent cylinder bore.

constriction just part of the system

Just how does the microscopic .030-.035-inch difference between a truly tight choke and a wide-open boring make such a marked difference in buckshot dispersion? Well, that tiny difference in diameter does not, in itself, make all that difference. It simply couldn't. The answer is that the choke is just part of a complex system that orders pattern development. Sure, choke constriction does play an important role; it is merely a static part of the pattern developing system. Just as vital are a pair of dynamic forces that work in concert with the constriction to shape the shot charge before setting it free.

The first factor is the pressure of the trailing wad on the base of the shot charge as it clears the muzzle and the second is the air resistance (drag) that works against pellets once they escape the controlling wad and powder gases. Buckshot pellets, encased in the plastic shotcup or simply loaded over a wad with a powdered plastic component known as Grex, go from a standing start in the chamber to a 1,100-1,200 fps mass in about 0.003 of a second. That puts a lot of pressure and momentum on the wad and pellets. The wad encounters the choke taper, which constricts it slightly – from .0729 down to .665 in an extra full-choked buckshot barrel. That, again, is not

The amount of choke constriction is just part of the system that determines an effective buckshot pattern.

much, but the tight choke does pinch down on the wad, slowing it and letting the shot charge escape with little or no pressure from the wad.

At the other extreme, a cylinder bore IC choke pretty much lets the wad slide through without being bothered, meaning it can remain nestled up against the base of the shot charge. A modified choke gives the wad a slightly tighter squeeze and improved modified comes down almost as hard as the aforementioned full choke. Thus, the way choke constriction slows the wad pretty much determines how the shot emerges from the muzzle – at which point it encounters air resistance. Air works harder against fast-moving objects than against slower ones and the pellets slow abruptly during the first few feet out of the muzzle.

Pattern and shot string formation depend on how powerful that rear wad pressure is. If it's heavy, as in the case of an IC choke, the charge is virtually pancaked between the opposing forces of wad pressure and air resistance and the pellets spread outward, widening the pattern. In a full choke the wad is slowed more noticeably. The choke constriction retards the wad and the pellet string narrows down to squeeze through the smaller opening. Pellets tend to spurt through a full choke because the narrowing is a minor obstruction. They thus escape in a longer line and, because the wad is delayed by the choke taper, the pellets continue on a straighter course because they are not being rammed from behind as in the case of the more open choke. This phenomenon is more pronounced at high altitudes where air is lighter. Patterns are tighter across the board at altitude due to the reduction of the air resistance factor in the described scenario. In a vacuum an IC choke would theoretically deliver 100 percent patterns due to the absence of air resistance. The pellets could travel straight ahead, their superior mass giving them the momentum to outrun the wad and its potentially disruptive impact from behind. Choke, then, is important only as it retards or fails to retard the wad and how it prepares the shot charge for its impact with air resistance.

know the limitations

I've hunted deer in areas that mandated the use of shotguns all my life, a few times where buckshot was de rigueur. Yes, I've been successful with buckshot and have no horror stories to relate about wounded animals or missed opportunities. Plenty of range testing, however, has convinced me that my success was as much a case of good fortune as it was prime — read short-ranged — opportunity. Sure, buckshot loads today are better than ever but as far as I'm concerned anything beyond 35 yards is a definite "maybe" with conventional lead loads, and with some load-choke combinations 20 yards might be too far. Every time I do a shotgun seminar I hear a few stories of buckshot bringing down bucks with 60- or 80-yard shots. Yes, it can be done by lucky hunters, but I'd never suggest it and ethical hunters shouldn't condone it.

Given the rapidity with which a single, semi-round pellet slows and thus sheds its energy, I have to say that the aforementioned 35-yard envelope is based more on ballistic surety than a luckily placed pellet. Again, with the right choke-barrel combination Hevi-Shot offers a significantly longer effective range. If you have to shoot lead buckshot or Hevi-Shot, absolutely, positively, do your homework. No relative, neighbor, magazine writer or store clerk can accurately tell you what load(s) your gun and choke will handle best. You'll probably be surprised how badly some sizes perform and how well others do. Try a variety of shot sizes *(Number 00 is probably the most versatile and effective)* and a variety of chokes *(extended chokes seem to outperform convention screw-ins)* before making a decision. And remember when patterning that a 10-inch pie plate is a far better judge of buckshot effectiveness than the traditional 30-inch circle. Also remember that regardless of pattern density a buckshot pellet has the ballistic coefficient of a bowling ball. It loses energy and effectiveness very quickly and with most loads beyond 40 yards your hopes of success are based on a very lucky strike from a stray pellet — definitely not a trait of an ethical hunter.

Lead buckshot comes in six sizes from Number 000 (10 pellets, .36 caliber in 3-inch shell), Number 00 (15 pellets, .33 caliber in 3-inch and 12 pellets in 2.75-inch shell), Number 0 (12 pellets, .32 caliber in 2.75-inch shell), Number 1 (20 pellets, .30 caliber in 2.75-inch shell, 24 in 3-inch shell) and Number 4 (41 pellets, .24 caliber in 3-inch shell, 34 pellets in 2.75-inch shell). The number of pellets may vary with manufacturer. American shotshell manufacturers usually reserve Number 2 and Number 3 shot for 20-gauge loads. Yes, buckshot is and always has been an effective load for deer hunting, but only in the hands of those who know and abide by the load's limited effectiveness.

Ohio farmer Dick Cochran is a big fan of the Remington Copper Solid slug.

Shotguns for Deer

state-of-the-art slug guns

For three-quarters of the 20th century small game shotguns became deer guns by simply changing the load. The market just wasn't big enough to warrant much innovation and manufacturers made few design concessions for slug or buckshot shooters. Ithaca Gun was the first shotgun company to cater to slug shooters, introducing its 12-gauge Deerslayer in 1959. The Deerslayer was a John Browning Model 37 bottom-ejection pump design that Ithaca pulled off the scrap heap when Remington discontinued its predecessor, the Model 17, in 1936.

A spokesman at the Remington Museum assured me that Big Green had willingly given up the design when the original Browning patent had run out to avoid any charges that Remington held a monopoly in the shotgun market. Ithaca Gun historian Walter Snyder, however, says that Ithaca Gun actually built a few Model 37s while Remington was still producing Model 17s and stored them until the patent expired. The original Deerslayer featured iron rifle sights on a straight-tube barrel (no forcing cones or chokes) with a tight .704-inch internal diameter barrel (conventional 12-gauge barrels are .729) that firmly squeezed all of the slugs available on the market that time.

"Tolerances were really strict," said former Ithaca Gun service manager Les Hovencamp. "I guess if a barrel came off the reamer at .705 or .706 it was scrapped." Most any slug on the market filled this bore, thus retaining the essential square-to-bore orientation before exiting the barrel. The result was vastly improved accuracy, even though the bore diameter was eventually bored out to .719 in the early 1980s to lessen pressures, as slugs got bigger. All major manufacturers eventually followed by offering optional "buck barrels"— shorter, open-cylinder versions of existing designs fitted with rifle sights.

The length of a slug barrel is of very little importance. You'll find that while the powder burns in the first 16 to 17 inches of the bore, there will be a slight increase in velocity up to about 25 inches. Anything longer than that actually begins to work as a brake on the ejecta, slowing it down. Most production guns come with 22- to 25-inch barrels while a few hand-built guns have 20-inch barrels.

Shotguns designed and manufactured specifically for slug shooting are a relatively new concept.

birth of rifled barrels

Rifled shotgun barrels have been used by trapshooters and produced by European designers for the better part of a century, but until BRI's Bob Sowash achieved a certified MOA group *(five shots measuring 1 inch center to center at 100 yards)* with his slug and a custom-rilled barrel in the early 1970s, the spiral spout was largely unheard of on these shores. In fact, until the 1980s federal law prohibited rifled barrels over .50-caliber for civilian use. They were deemed "destructive devices." The grandfather of rifled shotgun barrels is probably Olie Olson, head gunsmith for E.R. Shaw Barrels of Bridgeville, Pennsylvania, until his retirement in 2001.

A transplanted Californian living in the shotgun-only environs of Allegheny County, Pennsylvania, Olson was frustrated by the relative inaccuracy of conventional slug guns. He toyed with rifling shotgun bores with various twist rates in the late 1970s. When Shaw obtained permission from the feds to build spiral tubes for civilian shotguns in 1982, the door was opened for slug shooting to enter the 20th century. Shaw started producing rifled barrels that could be retrofitted to certain solid-receiver, fixed frame shotguns like High Standard Flite Kings. Today Randy Fritz's Tar-Hunt Rifles uses Shaw barrels on its custom bolt-action and pump slug guns and once toyed with the idea of importing today's version of the High Standard receivers from the Philippines.

Rock Barrels in Oregon and Pennsylvania Arms of Duryea, Pennsylvania, ventured into the fray early but the only company that would have a lasting presence was the Hastings Company of Clay Center, Kansas. Originally conceived as a barrel-maker for interchangeable choke systems, Hastings owners Phil Frigon and Bob Rott began importing rifled Paradox barrels from France in 1985 and quickly became the prime aftermarket source of rifled shotgun barrels. Hastings encountered very little competition in the aftermarket rifled barrel market until Ithaca Gun tested the waters in 2003. The venerable upstate New York gunmaker was famous for its "Roto-Forged" smoothbore barrels until its plant moved in 1989 and the forge proved too expensive to rebuild at the new facility. The company was outsourcing barrels for its own M37 pumps from 1989 to 2002 when it purchased a computerized barrel lathe and, for a brief time, marketed aftermarket barrels for other brands of shotguns. The lathe, however, was lost to a creditor when Ithaca closed its doors in New York in 2005.

There are conflicting schools of thought on rifling twist rates. An inarguable fact is that the faster twist rates *(one turn in 24 or 25 inches)* accentuate expansion of slugs. Hastings' Bob Rott and gun builder Mark Bansner say that they saw no difference in accuracy of sabot slugs between 1-28 and 1-36 barrels. Randy Fritz and Shaw's Olie Olson, however, claimed that the sabots preferred 1-28 and Foster slugs preferred 1-36 with 1-34, a good compromise for both. Fritz, who has been in on the development of Lightfields since their inception, actually

The advent of rifled barrels sparked a revolution in slug shooting.

Previous page:
The accuracy of today's slug guns, firing modern loads, is better than ever before.

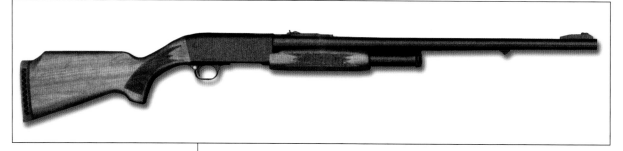

Introduced in 1959 the Ithaca Deerslayer was the first shotgun built specifically for slug shooting.

builds his custom guns with a special twist rate — I think it's 1-34 — to shoot Lightfield Hybreds. I have noticed that the soft Foster slugs, when spun too much (1-28 for example) seem to want to "flow" or fly apart due to centrifugal force. I have also noticed that guns with 1-28 twists (1-24 in 20-gauge) do seem to handle high-velocity slugs better than those with 1-36 twist rates.

twist rates (at 1,400 fps)

1-25 inches ......37,440 rpm	1-34 inches ....27,528 rpm
1-28 inches ......33,428 rpm	1-35 inches ....26,742 rpm
1-32 inches ......29,250 rpm	1-36 inches ....26,999 rpm

first production rifled barrels

Ithaca and Mossberg were the first companies to offer production guns with rifled barrels in 1987 — Ithaca with its Model 37 Deerslayer II and Mossberg introducing the Model 500 Trophy Slugster. Heckler and Koch started importing Benelli autoloaders and affixing them with Shaw rifled barrels. Thompson Center's custom shop and tiny New England Firearms (H&R) started marketing single-shot rifled-barrel guns in the very late 1980s. Today all major shotgun manufacturers — Remington, Mossberg, U.S. Repeating Arms, Browning, Ithaca, H&R, Marlin, Savage, Beretta, Benelli, Franchi and Traditions — offer at least one model with a rifled barrel. Although smoothbore shotguns and conventional slugs still make up nearly 65 percent of the retail market, rifled barrels and sabot slugs are the most advanced and accurate and represent the fastest-growing segment of the industry.

slug gun shortcomings

The effectiveness of a slug gun is limited by chamber pressure *(shotguns operate at less than 12,000 pounds per square inch, rifles up to 60,000)* and, due to looser construction, vibration. Vibration is not nearly as much of a factor with buckshot guns simply because the whole idea there is to spray a pattern of pellets as opposed to centering a single projectile. Slug guns definitely need to be more precise. That's why the bolt-action and break-action singleshot are the most accurate actions. The barrel is fixed (screwed) to the receiver and the entire function of the gun is in a straight line with nothing hanging off it, which means less barrel-shaking, accuracy-robbing vibration. That's also why today's slug barrels are typically short. A long barrel used to be an advantage since older powders needed more space to burn and efficiency was compromised by gas leaking past undersized wads. But the high-tech powders used to propel today's gas-sealing wads is burned in the first 16-17 inches of barrel length, so any barrel of at least 18 inches should be adequate in that respect.

The author took this 8-point buck with a Remington 11-87 autoloader. The autoloader, however, is the heaviest and inherently the least accurate of any slug gun design.

Slugs, like shotshells, thus gain nothing ballistically from a longer barrel. In fact, unlike shotshells, slugs have characteristics that may actually make the shorter barrels more accurate. Slugs are so slow that the gun recoils nearly 5/8 inch before the slug can get out the muzzle. Because of this phenomenon a longer barrel is actually detrimental to accuracy because the longer the slug stays in the tube the more it is affected by the barrel movement caused by recoil and vibration. Autoloaders are inherently the least accurate action because there is so much movement when the trigger is pulled. At ignition the gun starts recoiling, the bolt slides back to eject the empty hull and a fresh load is levered out of the magazine and up to where it can be slammed into the chamber by the returning bolt.

Pumps, with the fore end slide and magazine dangling from the barrel, which is loosely fitted to the receiver, also experience a great deal of vibration at ignition. Ithaca's Deerslayer II line, featuring a free-floating *(not attached to the magazine)* barrel that is fixed permanently to the receiver, is the only exception among pump guns. Although the single shot is the simplest design, it usually is a very inexpensive model shotgun with a less-than-bank-vault-solid lockup, heavy trigger and cheap barrel — factors that

Despite all the advances in slug guns and loads, the shotgun hunter will never achieve the range and effectiveness enjoyed by rifle hunters.

Above: A good barrel and a relatively light, crisp trigger are the hallmarks of a good slug gun.

Below: The bolt-action shotgun is the state of the art in slug guns.

negate the action's accuracy potential. Exceptions are the Mossberg SSi-One, the Thompson Center single shot that was phased out of its custom shop in the late 1990s and the H&R and New England Firearms *(identical except for wood and finish)* 980 and 925 *(20-gauge)* series. These guns used extremely heavy bull-barrels to tame harmonics and offset the effects of the heavy triggers. Mine were both hand-fitted at the factory to maximize the tightness of the lock-up and the triggers were tightened. The result is two simple but extremely accurate test guns that I've toted to deer stands on many occasions.

state-of-the-art slug guns

bolt actions

The state of the art in slug guns is the bolt action. Once the least expensive, simplest shotgun action, the addition of the rifled barrel and a few other amenities *(like fiber-optic sights, rifle-style synthetic stocks and scope mounts)* has turned the bolt from a beginner's gun into the most inherently accurate slug gun available. If you're old enough to have seen Vietnam "live" through binoculars or on the evening news or to have voted for McGovern, chances are you're familiar with the concept of bolt-action shotguns for beginners.

Who among we gray-templed outdoors types doesn't remember a sibling or crony who started deer hunting with a slug-loaded, inexpensive bolt action or single shot? Seems like there was always somebody with a Polychoked Mossberg 195, Marlin 55 or Sears 140 bolt gun. Or, by the same token, an Ithaca 66 Super Single – or even a crusty old uncle who put slugs in his "Long Tom" Marlin goose gun or one of the old break-action single-digit model H&Rs. Back then singles and bolts were "starters" reserved for kids, or they were multipurpose ordnance used by folks who weren't as serious about deer guns as they were in simply having something in the truck or the barn that could be of use in all seasons. The bolts and singles of those days were at the lower end of the shotgun spectrum. But you've also got to remember that shotguns and slugs per se weren't accurate back then, either. But, as I say, that was then – this is now. Today's bolt-action slug guns are definitely not reinventions of the wheel. Comparisons between them and yesterday's simple actions are about as valid as racing the *Spirit of St. Louis* against a Stealth bomber.

"Years ago the bolt action was simply an inexpensive shotgun with little more than reliability to justify its existence," said Mossberg CEO Alan "Iver" Mossberg, whose company was one of the prime providers of entry-level bolt shotguns decades ago. "The growing popularity of the pump and autoloading shotguns nearly retired the bolt action. Oddly enough, when bolt action

steadygrip

From the "What-Will-They-Think-of-Next?" Department comes Benelli's SteadyGrip system. The company's Super Black Eagle and M1 Field autoloaders offer optional stock system that consists of a soft-rubber coated pistol-style grip that drops away from the stock just behind the trigger guard at a 60-degree rear angle. The concept actually dates back more than a decade. In the late 1980s—before the formation of Benelli USA, when the Italian line came from Urbino to the United States through Heckler & Koch — the company's tactical shotguns were offered with a similar-looking "tactical" grip. But no one has ever put one on a sporter until now. Having extensive experience with M-16/AR-15s, which feature a grip and stock configuration virtually identical to the SteadyGrip, I was well aware of the advantage the system afforded off-hand shooting, but I'd also tried some aftermarket tactical grips on other shotguns in the past and found that their abrupt drop actually accentuated recoil when the gun was fired from a seated position.

It was thus with admitted skepticism that I first approached the SteadyGrip. But after a couple of range sessions and a week-long turkey hunt with the Super Black Eagle on the Nail Ranch in west-central Texas, I came away impressed. The rearward angle and soft rubber grip actually made the inertia system (recoil-operated) Benelli autos comfortable to shoot from a seated position — even when the Super Black Eagle was loaded to the tips with 3.5-inch, 2-ounce Federal Grand Slam turkey loads. The SteadyGrip-fitted guns weigh exactly the same and have the same stock dimensions (in terms of length of pull, drop at the comb and drop at the heel) as their conventionally stocked versions and are priced only moderately more. *(M1 SteadyGrip is $90 more than its conventionally stocked version; the Super Black Eagle just $80 more.)*

When shooting off-hand on the range, the SteadyGrip provided the familiar suppressed recoil and, well, steadiness I remembered from my Service Rifle competition days with the AR-15. In fact, the session engendered a mental note to pick up an optional rifled slug barrel (both the Super Black Eagle and M1 Field have them). Afterall, the SteadyGrip models of guns are drilled and tapped for scope mounting. The SteadyGrip system definitely makes the guns "dedicated use" ordnance. But while the SteadyGrip concept doesn't lend itself to comfortable wing shooting, it'll make a great companion in the turkey woods or deer blind.

interest was waning, many states were changing their deer seasons to "shotgun only," slug ammunition was improving tenfold. Suddenly the bolt-action was reborn and repositioned." But Mossberg's 695 was discontinued at the end of the twentieth century, leaving the Savage 210 alone in the genre. In the twenty-first century, however, used Browning A-Bolts were routinely selling for four figures and the company brought them back in 2011, just after Savage introduced the Savage 220F (20 gauge) in 2010 and the revamped 12-gauge 212 in 2011.

Marlin's 512 was the first-ever bolt-action rifled barrel gun, starting off in 1994. The story goes that veteran *Outdoor Life* shooting editor Jim Carmichel suggested to Marlin that a rifled barrel on its bolt-action Model 55 Goose Gun would be a big seller and thus it was born. The 512, which featured unique side-saddle scope mounts, a 1-28 twist rate in its 22-inch barrel and later a synthetic stock and fiber-optic sights, was discontinued due to slumping sales in 2001. The Browning A-Bolt slug gun, essentially that company's bolt-action rifle design chambered for 12-gauge, was probably the best-built production slug gun ever made, but it enjoyed a short life span, being discontinued in 1998 after just three years of production. The gun cost more than twice the price of the Mossberg and Marlin bolts and consumers just weren't willing to pay the difference. If you can find one today in good shape, grab it. The problem is that most people who have them know what they have and aren't going to part with them.

The Savage 210 Master Shot is similarly a rifle design (Savage's inexpensive but accurate 110 series) chambered in 12-gauge. Like the Browning, the Savage 210 uses a rifle-style bolt with front locking lugs and a 60-degree throw. The Mossberg and Marlin are shotgun bolts that lock up when the bolt handle is dropped into a recess cut into the stock. The Savage uses a synthetic stock that is virtually identical to the one on its bull-barreled varmint and tactical rifles, the exception being an integral box magazine that protrudes from the bottom of the receiver like a molded goiter. The Savage has a 24-inch rifled (1-35) twist rate with no sights. The

Above: **A rack of bolt actions** *(left to right)* **Savage 210, Tar-Hunt RSG-12, Marlin 512P and Mossberg 695.**

Below: **The Savage 210 bolt gun was replaced in the line with the clip-fed, Accu-Triggered 212 in 2011.**

receiver is drilled and tapped to accept scope mounts. Unquestionably, the ultimate in slug guns today is the custom-built Tar-Hunt RSG (Rifled Slug Gun) bolt-action series made by gun builder Randy Fritz of Bloomsburg, Pennsylvania. The RSG-12 Professional and its 20-gauge counterpart, the RSG-20 Mountaineer, are basically Remington 700 rifle clones chambered for shotgun loads. Fitted with Shaw barrels, Jewell triggers, McMillan composite stocks, Pachymar Decelerator recoil pad and the custom-made action, the guns retail for thousands. Fritz also fits custom barrels and does trigger work on Remington 870 pumps, calling that model the DSG (Designated Slug Gun) series.

single shots

Single-shot, break-open slug guns such as the H&R 980 and 925 Ultra Slugster (bull-barreled 12- and 20-gauge models) and Mossberg's 12-gauge SSi-One are similarly accurate but tend to be heavier and lack the quick follow-up of the bolt actions. Because the

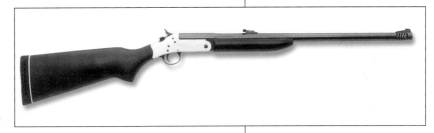

scope rail is mounted directly on the chamber, these guns also tend to be rougher on scopes. New England Firearms, the Marlin-owned sister company to H&R, makes the 980 in a less expensive version and both companies market (NEF Tracker and H&R Topper) light, compact single-shot versions with rifled bores. The very inexpensive Pardner series is a smoothbore version.

Above: The single-shot H&R Topper is available with a rifled barrel.

Below: The H&R 980's barrel is heavy enough to offset the effects of a heavy trigger-pull

New York hunter Roger Scales took this 13-point doe with an Ithaca Deerslayer using a Brenneke slug in 1994. It was one of the largest-racked does ever recorded.

The Benelli inertial recoil operating system used in the 12-gauge Stoeger Model 2000 slug gun permits the use of a wide range of $2^3/_4$- and 3-inch loads.

pumps

Pumps are the most popular slug guns, probably due to retail price point as well as their light weight, durability and simplicity. The compact, lightweight aspect of the pump makes it the darling of the stalker as well as the stand-hunter. Follow-up shots are easier with a pump than with any action other than an autoloader, but heavier recoil is the price one pays for light, compact design. There are nearly 10 million Remington 12-, 16- and 20-gauge 870s wandering around the country while the 12-gauge Mossberg 500 and 835 Ultri-Mag are among the sales leaders every year. Ithaca's M37 pump comes in several 12-, 16- and 20-gauge configurations for deer hunters, including the 11-pound 12-gauge bull-barreled Deerslayer III, which is available only by special order through the company.Ithaca Gun failed again in 2005 but resurfaced in Ohio under new ownership that changed the face of the company. The newest Ithaca Gun offers the old Deerslayer II but the newer Deerslayer III is a trimmed down version of the New York model, with a lighter bull barrel and new twist rate (now 1-in-28) that, coupled with the free-floating concept, leads outstanding accuracy.

The Browning BPS, Winchester SpeedPump, Benelli Nova, NEF Pardner and a couple of pumps from other companies offer rifled barreled versions.

autoloaders

The autoloader is popular due to its tendency toward lessened recoil and quick follow-ups. The trade-off is that they are generally much heavier and far more expensive than other actions. They are also more complicated and often less reliable and somewhat less accurate due to the excessive vibration caused by the cycling action. The Remington 1100 is the lightest and oldest autoloading model on the market and is available in both 12- and 20-gauge slug versions. It's a long time favorite with

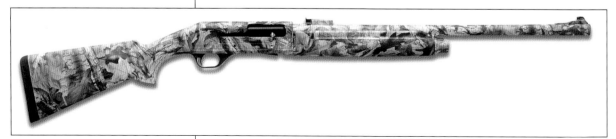

slug hunters, as is its successor, the 11-87 and the newer Versa, Browning's Gold, Silver and Maxus, Winchester's Super X2 and Super X3, Benelli's Super Black Eagle and M1 and Beretta's 12-gauge ES100 (formerly the Pintail), Weatherby's SAS and Traditions' Spanish-built XL-2000 autoloaders are all popular with slug hunters in both rifled barrels and smoothbores. Mossberg's 9200 fits that bill until it was discontinued in 2000, as was Winchester's 1400 a few years earlier.

doubles

Double-barreled shotguns, be they side-by-sides or over-unders, are notoriously inaccurate for slug shooting, since both bores often have their own point-of-aim. For that reason, no doubles are currently made with rifled barrels.

Double-barreled shotguns are notorious for shooting in two different directions and thus are not suitable for slug shooting. Occasionally a buckshot hunter will use a double for short-range shooting.

what's next?

In the late 1990s, with bolt-action shotguns well established as the state of the art, Remington director of firearms product development Jay Bunting told me that there would never be a slug gun built on the Model 700 rifle action. Bunting noted the whole industry learned a lesson through Browning, which built an excellent bolt-action gun based on its A-Bolt rifle action but with a $700 price tag it simply could not compete with the Mossberg, Marlin and Savage guns that were pouring out of mass merchandisers for less than half that price.

But when Remington brought out its 710 rifle in 2000, a bolt-action designed for Mart sales at $350 including a Bushnell scope, many of us thought the door was open for Remington to enter the bolt-action slug gun market with a competitively priced unit. "No, you won't see a 12-gauge 710," Bunting stated emphatically when questioned on the matter. "But how about a smaller gauge? How about one even smaller than 20 — a bolt gun designed around a very flat-shooting proprietary slug? Stay tuned." Intriguing.

Is Remington planning a proprietary smallbore slug gun built on the Model 710 rifle frame?

Recoil

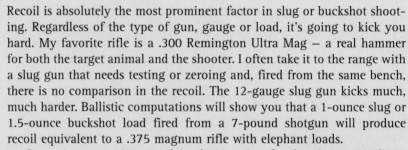

taming the beast

Recoil is absolutely the most prominent factor in slug or buckshot shooting. Regardless of the type of gun, gauge or load, it's going to kick you hard. My favorite rifle is a .300 Remington Ultra Mag – a real hammer for both the target animal and the shooter. I often take it to the range with a slug gun that needs testing or zeroing and, fired from the same bench, there is no comparison in the recoil. The 12-gauge slug gun kicks much, much harder. Ballistic computations will show you that a 1-ounce slug or 1.5-ounce buckshot load fired from a 7-pound shotgun will produce recoil equivalent to a .375 magnum rifle with elephant loads.

Getting someone interested in shotgunning for deer is not nearly as difficult as keeping them interested after they've been pounded by a shotgun. The good news is that there are ways to lessen recoil, which should be good news for all youngsters, women, small-framed men and even "tough" guys who won't admit to being intimidated by pile-driving stocks. One big step is to make sure that the firearm fits the user. Generally speaking, novices will be youngsters or women. Again speaking generally, they will be smaller-framed than the average adult male – for whom most firearms are designed. A small-framed person needs a smaller gun, one that is as user-friendly as possible. With slug and buckshot loads, shooting a gun that doesn't fit the shooter will result in much heavier felt recoil.

Virtually every manufacturer makes a shorter-stocked, thinner-gripped "youth" or even "ladies" model, usually in 20-gauge, with a trigger pull around 12 1/2 inches compared to the standard 14-plus. It is the ultimate folly to start a novice off with a heavy, big-bore gun and "let them grow into it." When teaching someone to drive you don't put the driver's seat back too far for them to reach the pedals and steering wheel in hopes that they will "grow into it" and it's just as important that they have a usable system to shoot. Yes, smaller people need smaller shotguns. But beware of that statement. If a gun has a lot of drop in the comb of the stock, the sensation of recoil will be even greater. Fitting squarely into that category are "youth" 20-gauge single-shot guns regrettably chambered for 3-inch loads. They may feel light to carry but that joy takes an immediate turnaround when the trigger is pulled.

A shotgun's recoil is intimidating to any shooter and must be dealt with.

Next page:
An inexpensive, lightweight single-shot is probably not the best choice for a beginning hunter due to its excessive recoil.

I've said it elsewhere in this book but it bears repeating here: Stay away from the economy-priced, lightweight single-shots. They are built to sell, not to shoot and the recoil they mete out can go a long way toward turning off any shooter. Granted, smaller shooters do need something with less weight to be supported by small arms; something with a shorter stock that keeps the center of gravity to the rear and affords a comfortable reach to the trigger.

Don't think that just cutting off the buttstock will solve everything. For one thing, just sawing off the stock will change the pitch of the gun, which could actually accentuate recoil. Be advised, the grip and forearm size is as important as stock length when fitting a shooter of smaller stature. A large grip in small hands doesn't allow sufficient thumb-over placement, forces the hand to stretch to reach the trigger and accentuates felt recoil. The problem we face is that smaller shotguns kick harder and recoil is something we're trying to control if not avoid. It is the single most intimidating factor in shooting. Manliness, unfortunately, is seemingly measured in foot-pounds, but I maintain that we shouldn't be reading testosterone on the chronograph. We should clear that up for novice shooters right away. Given the effectiveness of today's slugs and buckshot loads, the 20-gauge is no longer a popgun. It is a logical starting gun, given its reduced recoil and lack of heft.

Pump shotguns kick less than breechloaders only because they are marginally heavier, the added weight slowing the recoil reaction since the explosion simply has more mass to move. But while the pump is probably almost universally seen as the optimum starting gun, I see it as a common mistake. People like them because they are inexpensive, simple and durable. They are also light to carry, but the lack of heft translates into big recoil. My choice for breaking in new shooters would be to start them with an autoloader. Put load one slug at a time if you want to limit the new shooter's firepower but take advantage of that action's recoil, or gas-operated system to greatly reduce recoil. The reason they kick less than other actions is that in addition to being heavier, they are specifically designed to divert some of the energy generated by firing the cartridge into operating the shell ejection and re-chambering process. The energy that goes toward operating the action doesn't run rearward into the shooter's shoulder and cheek.

Yes, autoloaders cost more and weigh more. If you can get past the first, you can get around the second one. The Remington 1100 Youth Model, which comes in 20-gauge, is as light as most pump guns yet it has the recoil-absorbing quality of the autoloader. And, like most scaled-down models, the stock can be replaced by a conventional-sized stock if the shooter outgrows the original. Regardless of your choice of action, recoil can be tamed further in a couple of manners. An aftermarket recoil pad will likely be thicker and more efficient than the one that came with the gun. One new one comes from Sims' Limb Saver, a company that has virtually revolutionized the idea of dampening vibration on bows with a rubberized product of that name. This company is introducing recoil pads with large collapsible air pockets built in to work on the same principle as air bags in vehicles.

The Limb Saver recoil pads come fitted for specific guns, are easy to install, and effectively soften recoil better than anything I've ever tried. Recoil can also be reduced by installing mercury suppression cylinders, sometimes called "dead mules," in the buttstock or magazine of the gun. These simple but extremely effective items work on simple physics – a counterweight that blunts the rearward rush of the gun during recoil and spreads out the effect over a longer period of time. It's the same basic principle that's behind the gas cylinder in gas-operated autoloaders. Porting the barrel – having holes drilled in at least the top of the barrel near the muzzle to vent the gases before the slug leaves the muzzle – also serves to limit barrel jump and felt recoil.

Stock fit and its relation to felt recoil has already been mentioned, but no matter how well a stock conforms to the shooter, if the comb is too low to allow comfortable cheek placement while looking through the scope, a comb lift can be added economically. Leather, lace-on Monte Carlo pads are available through Cabela's, as are form pads from Beartooth that simply slide on or others that adhere to the stock. The reduced payload of the 20-gauge slug, of course, means less recoil than a 12 gauge but proper choice in ammunition is another factor. Lightfield Ammunition now has Lightfield Lites, a low-velocity *(about 1,300 fps)* 12-gauge slug designed specifically for less recoil. It's also very accurate in smoothbore guns with rifled choke tubes. Brenneke

Mercury recoil suppressors can be installed in the magazine of a shotgun to dramatically reduce recoil.

and Remington also offer low-velocity slugs for smoothbore guns and for the rifled-bore shooter; Winchester's BRI Standard Velocity sabots have been popular for that very reason since the mid-1990s. Above all we want the novice and shooter of smaller stature – and everyone else – to have a positive experience. That means making their slug guns as comfortable and user-friendly as possible.

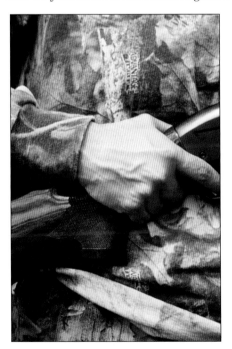

A gun must fit the user in order to lessen recoil. Stock length is not the only consideration – a smaller grip for smaller hands is equally as important.

custom slug guns

There are plenty of tinkering gunsmiths out there who, like previously mentioned Olie Olson at Shaw Barrels, were not satisfied with production guns and wanted something different. Most custom slug gun builders of my acquaintance are gunsmiths who simply improved existing production guns and possibly added a distinctive item or two that made the guns unique.

The only true custom slug gun builders — guys who built their designs from scratch — that I ever met are Pennsylvanians Randy Fritz and Mark Bansner. Both, not coincidentally, are custom rifle makers who branched into shotguns on a lark. Fritz, an international benchrest rifle competitor from Bloomsburg, builds a handful of his custom RSG-12 and RSG-20 bolt-action guns for police SWAT teams and a few truly serious hunters every year along with dozens of benchrest and hunting rifles. Bansner, a former U.S. Army armorer from Adamstown discontinued his SSG-1 bolt-action design in 1996 and now concentrates totally on custom hunting rifles.

Above: Custom gun builder Randy Fritz.

Below: Mark Bansner's SSG slug gun, a Tar-Hunt RSG-12 and a Marlin 512.

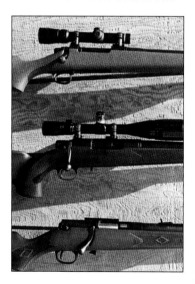

Bansner's SSG-1 actually predated Fritz's innovation and was its chief competition until the mid-1990s. The original 12-gauge Super Slug Gun was based on a Mauser action, Hastings Paradox barrel, Timney trigger and McMillan varminter stock. The second generation SS-1 went to High Tech synthetic stocks when Bansner bought the latter company in 1991. He then started machining his own actions and pillar-bedding them, leaving the 22-inch Hastings heavy barrels free floating. The 6$^1/_2$-pound gun used a Pachymar Decelerator recoil pad, a modified two-shot Marlin clip and is only chambered for 2$^3/_4$-inch loads. It was capable of MOA accuracy and sold for $1,200.

"I just couldn't afford to make them anymore," says Bansner. "People just saw it as a bolt-action slug gun, not a custom piece. When Browning, Savage, Mossberg and Marlin came out with bolt guns that shot very well, nobody was interested in a $1,200 custom gun. I had more invested in each action than the commercial guns retailed for." Fritz's Tar-Hunt RSG-12 is very expensive today but still gets enough interest to maintain an interesting sideline to his rifle work. He fills in the slow time by retrofitting Remington 870 pumps with permanently attached Shaw barrels and some trigger work, which results in a shooting system he calls the DSG-12 (or 16 or 20), for "designated slug gun."

In reality, the RSG-12 is only technically a shotgun. This is a 73-caliber Robo Rifle (the original looked like an M-788 on steroids) that, under the right conditions, can shoot sub-MOA groups with today's commercial high-tech saboted slugs. "I've always been fascinated with wildcats," says Fritz, a 30-year veteran of international benchrest competition. "Somewhere along the line I got interested in seeing how well I could make something as ballistically poor as a shotgun slug shoot — the ultimate wildcat." The "somewhere" that Fritz refers to was probably a three-year mid-1960s stay in Rochester, New York, where he worked for General Dynamics developing ground support systems for the F-111 tactical fighter plane.

A lifelong Pennsylvanian transplanted to the heavily populated Great Lakes plains, Fritz had to leave his .270 home and adapt to deer hunting with a municipally mandated slug-loaded shotgun. "When I moved back home I readily forgot that part," Fritz insists. He began building benchrest rifles on Remington actions in the early 1980s in his Bloomsburg, Pennsylvania, shop. But those frustrating years in the Rochester-area woods must have presented some sort of challenge because in 1988 Fritz drew up a prototype 12-gauge rifle. He sat down with Gayle McMillan in Phoenix, Arizona, in 1990 to map out the machining of the action and a suitable synthetic stock. He had Shaw Barrels turn some heavy-walled .728 ID one-turn-in-36-inch rifled barrels made of 4140 rifle steel in 1990 and had the first RSG-12s at the McMillan booth at the 1991 S.H.O.T. Show.

Fritz has achieved several sub-half-inch, 100-yard, five-shot groups with the 45-pound bench version of the gun and currently supplies barreled actions to all major slug manufacturers for their R&D work. The bolt still looks like a beefed-up version of its Remington cousin, only with two rear locking lugs in place of the Remington's series of lugs. The Tar-Hunt's two-piece bolt locks in the rear receiver ring rather than the front so that the nonrotating front half has room to incorporate a very narrow extractor cut in the actual chamber. The two stamped steel extractors are virtually identical to Marlin's and the ejector is a spring plunger type. The Tar-Hunt receiver is massive when one considers the modest chamber pressures of shotgun loads. Unlike commercial bolt shotguns, when the Tar-Hunt's bolt is closed its nose is covered completely by a heavy shroud to eliminate any possibility of gas escaping into the shooter's face.

"We wanted to err on the safe side. I've seen just changing lots of primers — not even brands — make a pressure increase of almost 3,000 pounds," Fritz says. "Federal guidelines only allow shotgun chamber pressures up to 11,500. Cases are only built to take 15,000." Since day one Fritz has used Shaw's 21.5-inch heavy barrels. While he'll build your Tar-Hunt in a variety of rifling twist rates, my gun was cut at 1-turn-in-28 inches, which is considered ideal for stabilizing sabot slugs. The interior diameter measures a SAAMI specs .728 in the grooves and .718 to the lands. The barrel walls are .120 inch thick while the Sniper or Tactical model Tar-Hunts sport straight taper .150-inch wall barrels. All Tar-Hunt barrels are ported 360 degrees at the muzzle to help loosen sabot halves on the exiting slugs, which apparently allows them to drop off simultaneously thus improving accuracy. The bolt was streamlined somewhat in 2001 and the guns are now fitted with M-700-style stocks with one-round blind magazines instead of 2-shot clips. The older style silhouette stock is now available as an accessory.

Mark Bansner's SSG custom bolt action *(left)*, pictured with a Tar-Hunt, was the only other original design, hand-built slug gun that the author ever saw. It was based on his own receiver design and fitted with a heavy-walled Hastings Paradox barrel and High Tech synthetic stock.

Your Shotgun

making it shoot better

What about accuracy in a slug gun? Sub-one-inch groups at 100 yards have been achieved by expert shooters under the right conditions with custom guns and saboted slugs. In the everyday world, with commercial ordnance and a weekend shooter, you'll find that anything inside of 5 inches at 100 yards is asking a lot from an out-of-the-box production slug gun. A slug gun and load that groups inside of 3-4 inches at 100 yards is a tack driver. Let's also understand that 100-yard target accuracy isn't essential to the average slug hunter. At 80 yards most of our shots fall inside a vital area twice the diameter of a basketball, hence an inch or two difference at 100 yards is moot.

Nevertheless, everyone wants their guns to shoot well. The good news is that virtually any shotgun can be made to perform better. In fact, almost all of them can be substantially improved. If you're going to shoot buckshot, the best way to improve your gun is to simply pattern different loads at the range or try different chokes. Barrel changes such as backboring, as noted previously, will probably not improve a buckshot pattern. Most die-hard buckshot shooters that I know put a sling on the gun and might gussy it up with fiber-optic rifle sights or a few even try illuminated dot scopes, but there isn't much more to do.

Bolt-action shotguns are inherently more accurate because they are produced with major accuracy-improving elements already encorporated.

slug gun barrels

With a slug gun, however, the barrel is the first consideration in improving your performance, the sole of any firearm. If you use your smoothbore barrel for other hunting and shooting, you can improve its performance by simply adding a screw-in rifled choke tube. Virtually every shotgun manufacturer now offers a rifled choke tube for its guns and there are plenty others on the aftermarket with Hastings leading the industry.

Next page:
The 12-gauge Remington 870 Super Slug is a dedicated slug gun that incorporates several unique accurizing features.

Adding a rifled choke tube to your smoothbore allows you to take advantage of the superior ballistics of sabot slugs.

One warning here: Don't try to shoot slugs through a barrel that is backbored (sometimes called overbored). These barrels have oversized internal dimensions that help them pattern shot better but they are too big for slug shooting, allowing the slug to tilt slightly as it travels down the barrel. Imagine how a tilting slug reacts when it hits the rifling. If the barrel is not backbored, however, a rifled choke tube allows you to use the high-tech sabot slug, which gives you a longer effective range and ballistic efficiency. Don't bother with sabots in a conventional smooth-bore, the super-expensive sabots are made to be spun by rifling and won't effectively shed their sleeves if they aren't spinning. Although some rifled choke tubes shoot well at 75-80 yards, common sense should tell you that imparting a 40,000-rpm spin on a slug that has already reached peak velocity when it hits the rifling is a lot less effective than spinning it from the chamber.

Remington shotguns are the darlings of the aftermarket as evidenced by all of the "custom" parts available for this 870 pump.

Next, make sure the twist rate is right for your particular load. The latest research shows a fast twist (1-in-25 in Badger aftermarket barrel or 1-in-28 available from Ithaca, Browning, Winchester, Benelli, Beretta, Franchi, Thompson Center or Marlin) stabilizes virtually everything, while the 1-in-34 or 35 twists in Remington, Hastings, Mossberg, etc., works best with conventional velocity (up to 1,500 fps) sabots and full-bore slugs. A slow twist like 1-in-36 is ideal if you're shooting only full-bore slugs. Most 20-gauge barrels have 1-in-24 to 1-28 twist. The old idea that longer is better in regard to buckshot barrels actually holds no water today. With today's loads, you'll see increased velocity with each inch of barrel length out to about 25 inches; after that the extra tube begins to serve as a brake. Extra long barrels are therefore a slight disadvantage for buckshot users, unlike waterfowlers or claybird shooters who want the extra length to aid in wing shooting.

pinning slug barrels

Regardless of the slug barrel you choose, pinning it fast to the receiver will make it shoot more accurately. Any barrel; any gun other than a bolt-action, single shot. Binding the barrel to the receiver *(have a gunsmith put a setscrew through the receiver wall to bear on the barrel sleeve)* will take a great deal of the accuracy-destroying vibration out of the system. Some guns will improve more than others when the barrel is pinned; depending on how tightly the barrel sleeve fits into the receiver to start with. But, as I said previously, any gun will benefit — I've seen pumps and autoloaders go from throwing "patterns" to tight "groups" with this treatment. To my way of thinking, the next step in any accurizing process for a slug gun is to lighten and stiffen the trigger. Even if your gun is a "buck special" with rifle sights and maybe a rifled barrel, it's going to have the same receiver, internal and trigger mechanism as its counterpart designed for scatter shot.

Pinning the barrel to the receiver lessens harmonics and is bound to improve the groups for any shotgun other than a bolt action or single shot.

A shotgun trigger is designed to be slapped, not squeezed like a rifle trigger, and gun companies' insurance carriers like to see substantial creep in triggers that are also set for a hearty slap. The fear is slam-fire on recoil and manufacturers err on the side of caution here. I don't care if you're the type who can crush cue balls with your fist, nobody can wring full potential out of a firearm with an 8- to 10-pound trigger pull. In a perfect world, we'd have slug guns with crisp 3-3.5-pound pulls, but in this world even a five- or six-pounder isn't bad so long as there's no creep. Hastings offers a readily adjustable drop-in trigger system for Remingtons but most gunsmiths can take the trigger down for you. Some guns can be adjusted more than others — Remingtons, Ithacas and Berettas are fairly adjustable; Mossbergs and Winchesters are not. Some gunsmiths don't want to work on triggers because of liability or the fact that such an adjustment voids the gun's warranty, but anybody who does work for trapshooters can and will do it for you.

Left: Having a gunsmith smooth out your trigger to lessen the pull weight and eliminate creep can go a long way toward tightening groups.

Below: Hastings at one time had gunsmith Allen Timney make a drop-in adjustable trigger system for Remington 870s. Today Timney Triggers makes a do-it-yourself 870 Trigger Fix.

another cure for inaccurate guns

The accuracy-destroying vibration that I've referred to is known as harmonics. While shots that wander around the face of a target or patterning board can be caused by a variety of factors, many are caused by the harmonics of the barrel. The barrel vibrates wildly in thin-walled shotguns more so than in rifles — barrels even "whip" a bit due to the concussion and the pressure of the ejecta flying down the tube.

The amount of vibration and severity of the whip are fairly constant, shot to shot, in a particular gun but ammunition typically isn't. You'll find that slugs commonly vary 10-50 fps, shot to shot, which means that the projectile is coming off the rifling when the barrel is in a slightly different position in the "whip" each time. That means, of course, that the projectile will impact in a different spot. The dampening effect that bull barrels have on harmonics is the reason they are so accurate; their weight lessens vibration and stiffness lessens the whip. But bull barrels are, by their nature, very heavy to carry in the field.

In recent years I've tamed barrel harmonics in several slug guns — not to mention a trap gun, a couple of rifles and a balky muzzleloader by having the barrels — and, in some cases the receivers, cryogenically treated. Knight Rifles now has its in-line muzzleloader barrels cryonized and many custom rifle builders do the same. Cyrogenic tempering — the deep freezing and deep heating of metals — changes the molecular structure, making it harder and stiffer. In many cases it also makes the metal less porous, which aids in subsequent cleaning. Cryogenics have long been used to temper tools, machine parts and cutters and more recently vehicle brakes, race car components, golf clubs, softball bats, tennis rackets and, yes, firearms barrels.

I'm not a metallurgist but I do know through personal application that cryogenic tempering has improved the performance of my guns and of others. Certainly some guns are helped more than others. With my guns in some cases the difference was negligible and in others there was a profound improvement. A lot depends on the initial quality of the barrel and its steel. Some rifle barrels are cut with a more meticulous, precision method or are cut from metal that has already been stress-relieved and don't need tempering to further relieve stress. That's not the case with shotgun barrels.

Alabama hunter Tony Nafe with a Texas buck taken with a Tar-Hunt 16-gauge DSG-1 pump gun and Lightfield Commander sabot slug.

Some friends of mine in the business are wary of cryogenics. After all, there is no visible difference in the metal after it has been cryogenically treated. Like those fish and game feeding tables in the newspapers, or fishing's Color Selector, or those little deer alert gizmos for your car, cryogenics has some folks who believe in it and others who scoff at the idea. One friend, with a background in chemistry and metallurgy, was a scoffer. He was also an AA trapshooter who'd bought a new high-dollar gun that simply didn't shoot well despite the fact that it had been cut to the exact dimensions of his old one. After three trips back to the factory, where he was basically told that there was nothing wrong with the gun, my friend reluctantly tried having the barrel cryogenically treated. He's right back to 100-straights and cryogenics has a new believer.

All firearms are produced with internal stresses. As the metal is bored, reamed and machined, mechanical stresses are created. As forgings and castings cool, the differing rates of temperature change introduce residual stresses. Even heat-treating leaves thermal stresses behind. As mentioned earlier, careful manufacturing produces barrels that shoot well, stresses and all. Cryogenic stress relief, however, can improve even the benchrest-quality barrels by relieving the internal stresses. It's those stresses, or weak spots, that cause barrels to twist and arc as they heat up from firing. That's why good three-shot rifle or slug gun groups are easier to get than good five-shot groups. Scatterguns do the same thing. At the end of a typical 10-shot trapshooting string, pattern placement can shift 6 inches in some shotguns. With 25 shots, pattern placement can shift up to 12 inches — a 40 percent change. At a very affordable cost, a cryogenic company will take a barrel down to minus-300 degrees Fahrenheit, hold it at that temperature for a predetermined time, then slowly bring it up through the cycle to approximately plus-300 degrees. There are several cyrogenic companies out there. I had 300-Below Cryogenic Tempering Services of Decatur, Illinois (www.300-below.com), do my work. They tell me that their process permanently refines the grain structure of a barrel at the molecular level to produce a homogeneously stabilized barrel.

They also say that carbon particles precipitate as carbides into a lattice structure and fill microscopic voids. This creates a denser, smoother surface that reduces friction, heat and wear. All I know is that it took a couple of slug guns that had exasperated me and I turned them into good shooters. The rifle barrels I had treated are slower to heat up on the range and clean much easier than before. To my way of thinking, cryogenics helps shotgun barrels even more than rifles. After all, there is a lot more whip in a shotgun barrel and the slug remains in the barrel a lot longer than a bullet does in a rifle, and is therefore more affected by harmonics.

shotgun stocks

With a few exceptions, you will discover that slug guns have shotgun stocks that are more suited to wing shooting than to sighting through a scope. Mossberg offers a unique adjustable comb system on its Model 500 pump but any stock can be brought to the correct cheek position with a strap-on Monte Carlo trap pad from Cabelas, a foam version from Beartooth or a stick-on adjustment from Cheek-Eze. You're going to find that many of the factors that need attention to make your slug gun shoot better are also things that trapshooters work with. That's why I look at publications that cater to trapshooters — *Shotgun Sports Magazine* and shooting sports supply outlets like Gamaliel (www.gamaliel.com) — to find items and gunsmithing services for slug shooting. For instance, both slug shooters and trapshooters seek lighter, crisper triggers; want to lessen recoil and barrel jump and want higher combed stocks. Gunsmiths or companies that perform those services can be found in such publications. My favorite trap gun, in fact, is an Ithaca Model 37 receiver fitted with a 28-inch vent-rib barrel, to which I added the honed-down trigger and Monte Carlo stock (fitted with a Sims recoil pad) from my Deerslayer II slug gun.

Lifting the comb on a shotgun stock can make it more comfortable to sight through a scope and effectively lessens felt recoil.

recoil reducers

There are a variety of recoil-reduction devices for shotguns. Mercury-filled tubes, often called Dead Mules, can be inserted in the stock or forearm of your shotgun and are very effective at suppressing recoil. There are also a variety of specialty recoil pads to add to the effectiveness. Barrel porting reduces felt recoil and muzzle jump while also having the effect of disturbing muzzle gases and allowing sabots to break away freely. Porting, crown polishing, trigger work and barrel pinning may be outside the abilities of your local gunsmith. Gunsmiths and services advertised in trapshooting publications, however, will know absolutely what you're talking about and what you need — and they'll be experienced in doing the work. So don't be discouraged about the performance (or lack thereof) of your current slug gun. The bad news is that right out of the box most slug guns won't be tack drivers but the good news is that most all of them can be made to shoot better.

Porting a barrel makes sabot slugs shoot more efficiently and lessens barrel jump and perceived recoil.

Shooting
using your slug gun

We had a deal. Dad promised to teach me the art of shooting if I survived the first 10 years of life — fair enough. Of course, there were certain other stipulations — mostly vows of good conduct, closer attention to personal hygiene, schoolwork and chores, lessened hostilities toward siblings, etc. — but to me age was the biggie. My 10th birthday arrived after about two days short of eternity and, following the obligatory birthday cake and feigned gratitude over new socks, I dutifully reminded Dad of our agreement. That sunny spring afternoon we packed his 16-gauge Savage and a fistful of rifled slugs into our old station wagon and headed down the dirt road to the neighbor's farm. Years of helplessly watching family hunters come and go; of pressing my nose against windows of gun stores; of staring into gun cabinets and poring over the pages of gun magazines, melted away in the half-mile trip to Max's back pasture.

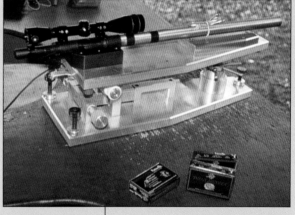

A remotely fired "rail gun" like this one takes the human factor out of accuracy testing a load.

After rudimentary instruction on the safe handling of a firearm — which I more or less ignored in the excitement of the impending moment — we reached what shall be romantically referred to as the moment of truth. It was time to touch one off. The target was a coffee can perched on a fence post about 20 yards away. I wrestled the 9-pound gun to a rest on a stump, sighted down the barrel at the brass bead and gave the trigger a quick, excited yank. My next recollection was of being sprawled on the ground, dazed with my bicep bruised and throbbing. To find my nose, one could follow a smeared blood trail across my youthful visage to a heretofore-vacant area seemingly somewhere above my right eyebrow. "You missed." — Dad's voice was barely perceptible over the loud ringing in my ears. "If you're going to try it again, hold it tighter against your shoulder and lean into it — like I said the first time," he remarked, apparently oblivious to my condition.

Dad was into the old "sink or swim" theory — today they call it aptitude testing. He would lead you to a certain point, but always let you experience the situation firsthand. You were the judge. If you wanted to

continue, he was there to instruct and guide — if not, he didn't force the issue. When I reached for the gun again that day he knew that he had my undivided attention and launched into a full-blown course on safety and proper shooting techniques. I was, needless to say, a model student.

Today I shoot thousands of slugs off a bench every year as a means of gainful employment and every session brings back the memory of the first. Shooting a slug gun from a bench is a brutal, bone-jarring, tooth-rattling and humbling experience, but it's not all fun — it takes finesse, experience and more than a little know-how to shoot accurately and get dependable results. That's why, whenever someone asks me what kind of accuracy he or she should expect from a specific gun or load I have to hesitate. "How should I know?" is the most honest answer, although I usually dance around the issue a bit rather than appear flippant. My stock diplomatic reply is that the achievement by Winchester and Remington ballisticians using saboted loads of 50-shot, 100-yard groups that measured slightly less than 3 inches were the result of performing their tests in climate-controlled tunnel ranges using custom-built, hand-lapped, air-gauged rifled barrels and actions which were bolted to a shooting platform and bench.

It should come as no surprise that you might obtain different results even when using the same load. Particularly if your test is conducted using an open-sighted smoothbore pump gun resting on a rolled-up jacket on the hood of your pickup in the local gravel quarry. Don't laugh; the majority of "accuracy tests" are conducted in a manner that tells the shooter nothing — even though he or she doesn't realize it. Slug guns and loads may have progressed markedly in the last 10 years but shooters haven't. So how should a slug gun be tested or sighted-in?

First let's put egos aside and admit that as much as we all like to think of ourselves as pretty fair marksmen, pinpoint 100-yard target accuracy is simply not readily achievable by the average hunter, regardless of the slug or gun. There are simply too many variables involved in shooting for the average shooter to honestly define the accuracy of a particular barrel or load by simply squeezing off a few rounds. The biggest variable is, of course, the shooter. Today's slugs are more accurate than most shooters. We know, for instance, that race cars can run laps in excess of 230 mph at the Indianapolis Speedway but 99 percent of American drivers couldn't get the pole sitter's car past 120 mph without crashing. It's the same with shooting. There are a few true experts who have the experience and ability to wring the absolute potential out of a gun or load, but the rest of us rely on various degrees of approximation and luck. Even when you're experienced it's possible to mess up. I shoot more rounds in a year than the average hunter fires in a lifetime, yet my technique is the first suspect when a gun or load isn't grouping well. There have been many times when a load wouldn't tighten inside of 3 inches at 50 yards and I was on the verge of writing it off as just another hollow claim. Then I made a minor technique adjustment and put the next several shots in one hole.

Accuracy is a relative term and the results of a shooting session depend on a wide range of factors.

Previous page:
The accuracy of a gun and load depends largely on the knowledge and skill of the shooter.

a solid rest

Variables? Well, one big one would be the rest. Is it solid? Can you make minute adjustments without torquing the barrel? Is the forearm rest soft enough to absorb the initial vibration at ignition? No, a rolled-up jacket on the truck hood isn't a good enough rest. You need a well-padded, rock-solid rest and sufficient padding to absorb the recoil, because there is going to be plenty of recoil and if it affects you, it will affect accuracy. A shotgun recoils more than a half-inch while the slug is still in the barrel and any vibration can affect accuracy. Even a loose magazine cap can throw slugs off by a matter of a couple of inches at 100 yards. Imagine the effect if you rest a pump gun on its slide when you shoot.

Good shooting calls for more than a good position on the bench and a general knowledge of the sight picture. It takes practice to apply the same gradually increasing pressure to the trigger until the breaking point on each shot. As noted previously, there are few variables more dynamic in the accuracy equation than trigger pull. A crisp (no creep), predictable, relatively light trigger is a necessity if you want to be able to coax the absolute accuracy potential out of a given shotgun load. You have to be thoroughly familiar with the trigger's breaking point in order to get any kind of consistency when shooting from a bench.

When chronographing the velocities of sabot slugs, the author encases the chronograph in a $^3/_4$-inch wood panel box to protect it from the ravages of flying sabot sleeves.

shooting advice

Randy Fritz, a Pennsylvania custom slug gun builder and world-class benchrest marksman, has shot half-inch, five-shot groups at 100 yards using his Tar-Hunt slug gun and commercial saboted slugs. Randy suggests the following routine when shooting slug guns off a bench:

- Use a quality rear bag and line the recoil pad of the gun directly over the back edge of the bag.
- Keep the front sling stud 2 inches forward of the front bag.
- Pull back firmly on the pistol grip with the right hand.
- Use the left hand (just behind the rest) to pull the forearm downward and rearward at the same time.

Wait a minute. We've all seen experts shooting rifles off benches with the gun's forearm lying on the front bag and the shooter's left hand tucked in front of him on the bench. "Those guys aren't shooting 600-grain loads," Fritz explains. Tuck that left hand underneath when shooting a slug gun off a bench and you're likely to be using it next to wipe a bloody brow. A 7-pound, 12-gauge slug gun exerts approximately the same felt recoil as a .375 magnum rifle and a thin-walled shotgun barrel will kick more wildly than a sleek rifle barrel. Also, if you sight-in a gun from the bench without pulling the grip toward you and the fore end down and to the rear, you're going to find that the gun shoots low when you shoot off-hand. Besides, if it's a pump gun you're trying to sight-in, there's no way you can get an accurate reading if the pump handle is lying on the front rest when you squeeze the trigger. A pump's slide mechanism is extremely unstable and you've got to be gripping it with your front hand – lying on the rest, of course – or the vibration will throw slugs all over the paper.

When shooting a shotgun from a bench, grasp the forearm and draw it down toward the bench on a 45-degree angle. This will give you a better recoil setup and a better reading on the accuracy of the load when you fire it freehand.

I like to rest a pump's receiver on the bag rather than the slide. There are also plates that clip onto a pump's tubular magazine and give the gun a flat, solid platform to rest on the front bag. Okay, we've discussed technique. Now you've got to understand the ordnance in order to make an accurate appraisal of its performance. How about the barrel? What is the twist rate of the rifling? As mentioned earlier, the conventional 1-turn-in-34-inches rate is a good compromise for shooting both sabots and full-bore slugs in 12-gauge guns. One-in-35 or 36 (pretty much the industry standard) is better for Foster slugs inside of 65 yards and 1-in-28 (Marlin and Benelli) has been found best for saboted ammunition out to 100 yards and beyond.

keep it simple

A quality adjustable rest and rear bag make a sighting-in session with a shotgun much more efficient.

One concession the average slug shooter should make is to shoot at 50-yard ranges rather than 100. The slug is simply vulnerable to the elements twice as long at 100 yards and the human variable is magnified appreciably in that second 50 yards, making it much harder to make accurate judgments. In fact, I shoot bore-sighted guns at 20-25 yards until they are centering the group, then move to 50 to tune for accuracy. If you sight-in at 100 yards one day even a slight change in wind direction or velocity will throw the group in an entirely different direction the next day.

To illustrate this, consider that an 8-10 mph crosswind, hardly more than a gentle breeze, will move a 1-ounce, 1,450 fps slug 5-8 inches off target at 100 yards. If you can manage a decent group in that wind, you'll have 5-8 inches of correction dialed into your scope. What happens if the wind dies – or worse yet – shifts 180 degrees the next day?

Chances are your slug won't be close enough to the deer to spook him. So do your work at 50. Even at that distance, the wind mentioned above will move that slug at least 2 inches off line, but it's not nearly as difficult to read or correct. If you are shooting conventional-velocity (1,400-1,500 fps) sabots, sight them in 2.5 inches high at 50 and they'll be dead-on at 100.

Truly high velocity sabots (1,700 fps and faster) should be sighted in 3/4-inch high at 50 to be dead-on at 100 yards or 1.5 inches high at 50 to be dead-on at 125 yards. When we hunted pronghorns with slugs on the wide-open plains of Wyoming we sighted our Winchester Partition Gold slugs 1.5 inches high at 50 and found them to be dead-on at 150. If you're shooting sabots with the correct twist rate, once you get a combination shooting in the same hole at 50 yards rest assured it will group well at 100. If you're grouping full-bore slugs well at 50, count on similar groups out to 75-80 yards.

Always, always be sure to re-zero your gun every year, even if you are going to use the same slugs as last year. As we've already seen, how you stored the slugs over the off-season may affect their point of impact and you don't know how the "new" slugs you bought off the dealer's rack this year have been stored, or how long. Just because one particular brand or type of slug shot well for you last year, the same slug bought off the shelf this year may shoot to a different point of aim — in fact, it probably will. Loads are constantly being tweaked, year to year, particularly with the smaller manufacturers.

slug deflection

Shotgun slugs have long been described as the ultimate "brush busters." Never mind the brush in front of that buck, with a slug you can just whack him. The big, slow slug will plow through the brush without deflecting. Well, it's not quite that simple. Any projectile fired through brush will deflect — any of them! Conventional wisdom holds that a high-velocity, low-caliber bullet will be more easily and more radically deflected by brush than a hulking, slow big-bore bullet — and to some degree that assessment is accurate.

The shape, construction and nature of the shotgun slug determines just how vulnerable it will be to deflection by brush. Obviously, for testing purposes, all brush isn't the same consistency or stiffness. Imitation brush must be constructed. A couple of big-name rifle writers have conducted deflection tests using several rows of $1/4$- and $3/8$-inch wooden dowels standing upright in 2x4 bases. Targets were placed three feet behind the rows of dowels and at 10 feet behind. They fired a variety of rifles from .22-250 to .30-30 to .375, 3 shots with each through fresh "brush." The results were, as you might figure, mixed. After all, a bullet with a pointed or rounded nose will veer at a different angle each time, depending what point of the ogive strikes the

Although slugs have been called the ultimate "brush busters," if you're shooting at this deer, the slug is going to be deflected somewhat by the brush.

dowel. But the tendencies showed that the high-velocity, low-weight bullets were far more easily deflected. The big, slow blunt-nosed, 250- to 400-grain bullets tended to deflect less. I tried the same thing with slugs, the forest of dowels with staggered targets behind them — the works. The only definite thing that I gleaned from the test was that it was a pain in the ass that called for lots of silly work, drilling and placing the dowels, then replacing them again, and again, after every shot.

The results were all over the place. As in the rifle tests, however, a pattern did emerge in terms of the shotgun slugs' deflection tendencies. Foster slugs, which are about as long as they are wide, tended to deflect slightly less than Brenneke-style attached wad slugs, presumably because of the latter's longer axis. Surprisingly, slugs fired through rifled bores also seemed to deflect less than the longer attached wad slugs did through smoothbores, presumably because the rotation helped the projectile maintain stability better than the static nose-forward design. A little asterisk is needed here, however, since the conventional hourglass-style sabot slugs, which spin at about 37,000 rpm, tended to deflect worse than any slug in the test. My theory is that their length and shape made them far more vulnerable to disruption. Modern high-velocity sabots like the Winchester Partition Gold, Remington Core-Lokt Ultra and Hornady H2K, being short, stout pistol bullets rotating at very high rpm, didn't deflect nearly as badly.

Unfortunately for slug gun hunters, whitetails in forested areas don't always present an unobstructed target.

An oddity was the Lightfield Hybred slug, essentially a Brenneke-style attached wad design that spins out of its sabot sleeves. It was the least prone to deflection other than the Foster slugs. Apparently the spin was a more positive effect on the slug than its length was a negative. That resistance to deflection is the reason SWAT teams like to use shotgun slugs to shoot through windows or vehicle windshields, mediums that will drastically deflect any rifle bullet. For instance, if a police sniper wants to shoot someone through a closed window, it entails two guns shooting at slightly different tangents. The first fires to shatter the window and the second shooter fires on report at the now-exposed target. Whenever Randy Fritz does a demonstration for prospective law enforcement customers for his Tar-Hunt slug guns, he shoots from 50 yards through $^{15}/_{16}$-inch-thick tempered plexiglass — the same stuff they use as bullet proof shields for drive-up bank tellers. The slugs cut neat, round holes through the glass without shattering it and without deflecting much at all, often less than 2 inches off line in a human silhouette set 5 feet behind the glass.

The reason, Randy theorizes, is that the soft nose of the slug simply yields (flattens slightly) upon impact instead of pivoting the slug on its nose like a pointed bullet would. The slug's mass then simply follows the nose through the medium. I guess the moral for shotgun hunters is that if the deer is standing close enough to the deflecting brush, you're probably going to hit him relatively close to the point of aim. If he is 10-15 yards behind the brush, you are better off with a short, fat slug design and a little luck. Besides, if the brush is open enough for you to see him, there must be a hole big enough to shoot through to avoid deflection.

bucking the wind

Wind is an abstraction, a ghost that works its mischief on a slug with unpredictable suddenness. We can't see the wind or the slug in flight so it is difficult to perceive the interaction of the two but the effect of wind is just as predictable as other ballistic phenomena. There are actually several factors working on any projectile as it flies downrange. Certainly gravity affects the flight, as does the wind velocity, density and direction. Momentum, figured off the velocity and mass of the bullet, and the aerodynamics of the projectile itself are also major factors. The amount of time that the projectile is in the air and the surface area of the projectile also come into play.

Generally speaking, slower velocity, bulky (short and fat with low BC) projectiles like shotgun slugs will be more drastically affected by the wind than a sleek, fast bullet. For example, a 1-ounce shotgun slug fired at 1,500 fps at a 100-yard target will be pushed 6-8 inches (depending on the shape of the slug) off line by a 10 mph crosswind. That's just a gentle breeze. By the same token, a 130-grain .270 bullet fired at the same time at the same target will move a little less than a half-inch off line under the same conditions. The rifle bullet is traveling nearly twice as fast and its sleek design keeps it from slowing as quickly as the bulky slug. Interestingly, a .22-caliber rimfire bullet and a 12-gauge shotgun slug — certainly opposite ends of the mass and weight scale — react similarly to wind, but for totally different reasons. The rimfire bullet's extremely small weight combined with its slow velocity make it very vulnerable to the wind. As noted previously, the slug's slow velocity and considerable surface area make it just as vulnerable.

"You'll find that some of the drift factors are multiplied when dealing with a really slow projectile like a shotgun slug," says custom slug gun builder Randy Fritz of Bloomsburg, Pennsylvania, one of the leading authorities on slug ballistics and performance. "If you have a right-to-left wind the slug will move not only left (on the target) but will also begin to print higher so the movement is actually up and left. If the wind is blowing left to right the slug will move right and slightly downward. It's a factor of the low velocity and the right-hand spin imparted on the slug by the rifling." A little knowledge like this, and experience, can allow a slug shooter to make adjustments in the sight picture to compensate. Regardless of the firearm or projectile, the effect that various factors have on flight can be corrected using the age-old common-sense techniques of Kentucky

Knowing the range and how much the wind speed is likely to affect your slug is essential when shooting at longer distances on windy days.

dealing with mirage

Another factor that'll send you packing when shooting at 100 yards is one that rifle marksmen fight and learn to read — mirage. It's a phenomenon that may well have nailed you without your knowing it. For instance, did you ever pick a "perfect" slug-shooting day; a windless, warm, high-sky day when you figured slug flight wouldn't be affected? You know the routine. You know your gun. It's a dead-calm day, your trigger control is perfect but the gun won't group worth a damn.

You'd stored the slugs in a climate-controlled area; made sure they were the same lot number that shot so accurately last time out. The scope is absolutely zeroed for 100 yards and the rings and bases torqued tightly; trigger is set at a crisp 2.5 pounds; you've got a rock-solid rest with an easy-to-move rear bag. Hell, the planets are in line for that career-best group. You are in fine shooting form, steady pressure on the trigger, gun drawn tightly to you. The trigger breaks smoothly right where you expected. And that "career-best" group you were seeking turns into a 5-inch roller coaster lateral spread. You try again and get the same deal — a little vertical deviation but a wide horizontal dispersion.

In a huff you pick up your equipment, slam it into the trunk and get behind the steering wheel, where you sit and stew; perplexed, angry, lost. If the dog is along, you swat him a couple of times just so your misery has company. What the hell is wrong? Mirage. You know, heat waves that you see coming off asphalt, vehicle hoods, rooftops on hot days. It rises from the sun-baked ground and you'll also commonly see it through the scope as it rises off rifle or shotgun barrels after a few quick shots heat the barrel 20-30 degrees over the air temperature. In fact, barrel heat and the resultant mirage is as much of a problem on a cool fall day as it is in the summer heat because of the temperature difference between the barrel and the air.

That shimmer actually bends the image you're looking at; typically moving the image higher and left or right, depending on the breeze. Your best bet is to shoot on calm, overcast days and to mount the target at least 30 inches above the ground and on grass, never on a stone, concrete or asphalt slab. Barrel heat isn't a major problem with conventional velocity slugs so long as you give it some time between shots. High-velocity slugs heat things up much, much faster and you will typically need to rest the barrel a couple of minutes between shots after the first couple. Also, shoot three-shot groups rather than five like benchrest shooters. Given the effects of recoil, barrel harmonics, mirage, etc., three shots will give you a better reading than five since the extra shots simply provide more room for the demons to ply their trade.

windage *(moving the point of aim off target to the windward side of the target)* and Arkansas elevation *(holding above or below the target, based on range)*. A shooter must keep in mind several factors or have sufficient hands-on experience to efficiently apply these techniques.

I once shot a caribou in Labrador at a laser-measured 162 yards with a stiff (I estimated it at 30 mph) crosswind. The bull was standing broadside, with his head to the left and staring at me, but I was only able to see his head, neck and back because the rest of his body was out of sight below the ridgeline. I placed the crosshairs on the base of his antlers, shifted them laterally to a point above the tip of his nose and carefully pressed the trigger. As I watched he buckled, trotted for about four or five steps and toppled over, the slug having taken him low in the lungs, more than 3feet to the right and below my line of sight over the horizon. That shot was a prime example of the use of Kentucky windage and Arkansas elevation combined with a knowledge of just how far that slug would drift under these particular conditions.

The correction could also have been made mathematically. Knowing the Lightfield Hybred slug's ballistic coefficient and that the load sported a muzzle velocity of about 1,450 feet per second and the wind was about 30 mph, the whole thing could be extrapolated to show that the slug would drift 42 inches. You can plug those factors into a good computer ballistics program and that binary brain can spit out the figures. But the *Hornady Handbook of Cartridge Reloading* also shows how to figure it without a computer.

As mentioned earlier, one must determine lag time in order to properly predict wind drift. The *Hornady Handbook* notes that cross-range wind velocity refers to the speed of the wind blowing perpendicular to the direction of fire. For most calculations the up-range or down-range components of wind velocity are of little consequence and need not be considered. The *Handbook* makes things simple by pre-calculating the lag time for various ballistic coefficients at most practical muzzle velocities, using a direct cross-range (90 degrees) wind velocity of 10 mph. The tables are to be used as guidelines.

The author took this Labrador caribou at 162 yards in a 30 mph crosswind using a Lightfield Hybred slug.

A very quick computation can be made by finding the closest BC, running across to the closest muzzle velocity and closest distance and multiplying the drift figure by the number of times 10 mph goes into it. For example, if the wind is blowing 20 mph, double the drift figure. This is merely a quick approximation and should be adequate for about 2 MOA if the component figures are accurate. However, the *Hornady Handbook* and most computerized ballistics programs also show formulas that allow the shooter to interpolate exact wind effect *(figured by the angle of the wind if it isn't a direct 90 degrees)* and exact BC if the shooter's bullet doesn't precisely fit the BCs listed.

A little knowledge on what factors affect your slug's flight and how your particular load reacts to those factors can solve a lot of problems when shooting at game.

wind drift comparison of common hunting projectiles
(approximate wind drift in inches)

bullet: .22-250, 55gr, muzzle velocity of 3,600 fps

crosswind	100yd	150yd	200yd	300yd
10 mph	1.0	2.3	4.2	10.2
20 mph	1.9	4.5	8.0	19.0
30 mph	3.1	7.0	11.9	31.2

bullet: .270, 130gr, muzzle velocity of 3,050 fps

crosswind	100yd	200yd	300yd	400yd
10 mph	0.7	2.9	6.9	12.8
20 mph	1.5	6.1	14.1	25.6
30 mph	2.2	9.1	22.0	38.0

bullet: .30-06, 165gr, muzzle velocity of 2,800 fps

crosswind	100yd	200yd	300yd	400yd
10 mph	0.8	3.4	8.0	14.8
20 mph	1.5	7.0	16.4	29.4
30 mph	2.5	11.1	25.1	44.9

bullet: 7mmMag, 162gr, muzzle velocity of 2,900 fps

crosswind	100yd	200yd	300yd	400yd
10 mph	0.6	2.4	5.7	10.4
20 mph	1.3	5.1	11.3	21.2
30 mph	1.9	7.3	17.8	33.1

bullet: 12-gauge shotgun slug, 440 gr, muzzle velocity of 1,500 fps

crosswind	100yd	150yd	200yd	300yd
10 mph	6.9	15.0	25.5	52.8
20 mph	15.0	31.2	52.1	105.0

bullet: .50 conical (muzzleloader), 425gr, muzzle velocity of 1,300 fps

crosswind	100yd	150yd	200yd	300yd
10 mph	7.2	15.0	25.2	52.4
20 mph	15.1	33.0	52.0	107.1

Plastic sabot sleeves have imbedded themselves in the protective 3/4-inch plywood box that the author built around his Oehler chronograph.

Optics for Shotguns

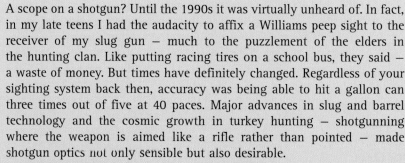

who needs optics?

A scope on a shotgun? Until the 1990s it was virtually unheard of. In fact, in my late teens I had the audacity to affix a Williams peep sight to the receiver of my slug gun – much to the puzzlement of the elders in the hunting clan. Like putting racing tires on a school bus, they said – a waste of money. But times have definitely changed. Regardless of your sighting system back then, accuracy was being able to hit a gallon can three times out of five at 40 paces. Major advances in slug and barrel technology and the cosmic growth in turkey hunting – shotgunning where the weapon is aimed like a rifle rather than pointed – made shotgun optics not only sensible but also desirable.

I've got good friends in the firearms industry who say in print that they get the same accuracy up to 100 yards with open sights and with scopes. Understand that they are expert shooters and have keen eyesight. I also suspect that they are embellishing the truth just a bit. I only know that not long after my 40th birthday my arms grew too short for me to read the newspaper and needed some sort of correction. Not long after that I had to retire from service rifle competition because of the fog that began to obscure the iron sights. Groups that I fire today with open sights aren't nearly so tight as those shot even with a low-magnification scope on the same gun. To my way of thinking, you'll never be able to realize a gun's or slug's potential unless you can aim extremely fine.

A fine whitetail buck lurks in thick cover. Optics can help you pick out the open spot to make a shot at this buck.

a consideration

Be advised, however, that shotguns don't contain their concussion in the receiver like rifles do and therefore punish a scope more than does a rifle. A $39.95 blue-light special isn't likely to last long on a shotgun in the deer woods. Since many shotgun hunters are new to the concept of putting a scope on their gun, they are unaware that just any scope won't do. In fact, whenever I do a seminar on slug shooting I suggest that the shooter pay at least as much, if not more, for the scope as he or she does for the shotgun. Invariably they look at me like a calf looks at a new gate.

Next page:
Scopes are a necessity on modern slug guns, not only for shot placement but also to take advantage of the accuracy potential of today's loads.

But think about it. The gun is worth nothing if the scope doesn't perform. If those optics fail or can't sufficiently determine a target for you, the gun becomes as useful as a tomato stake. Yup, the old theory that a slug gun is just a cheap rifle and therefore is worthy of a cheap riflescope is another misguided notion.

A good example came when I was shooting the newly designed H&R Model 980 bull-barreled slug gun with a factory rep shortly before it was introduced to the public. The company had a load of inexpensive 3-9x variable scopes from a popular manufacturer that they were thinking about packaging with some of their rifles. As we shot the 980 that day, a gun that is notoriously rough on optics due to the fact that the design dictates scopes must be mounted directly on the barrel, we destroyed at least a dozen of those scopes, each blowing apart internally after three to five shots. It was raining scope turrets and tension springs constantly and we got used to seeing more "Xs" than crosshairs. Price isn't the only determining factor. Some expensive scopes simply aren't suited to shotgun use, either.

A major magazine once commissioned me to do a slug test article and requested that I use a high-power target scope for the test session. A major manufacturer, seeking exposure in the big magazine, offered a pair of 6-18x target scopes with adjustable objectives — $500 models — to use for the test. The first scope lasted about 25 shots before it blew out of adjustment and wouldn't return. The second might have gone slightly longer but eventually met the same fate, forcing me to use a much lower powered scope, one built especially for slug guns, to complete the test. On the other hand, the most comprehensive accuracy testing I've ever seen was done with a 24x Leupold mounted on a Tar-Hunt custom 12-gauge and it held up well.

specialty shotgun scopes

It takes a good quality scope to resist shotgun punishment, and the shooter is wise to use one that is designed specifically for shotguns. Every major scope manufacturer makes at least one model specifically for shotgun — specialty optics built much sturdier than conventional riflescopes, usually focused to be parallax free at 50 yards rather than 100 or 150 like centerfire riflescopes. Partly because they tend to be lower-magnification, shotgun scopes typically offer longer eye relief, a major consideration for anyone who'd rather not have his eyebrow dented by the scope on these notoriously heavy-kicking guns.

The ideal long eye relief slug- or buckshot-hunting setup would likely be a suitable scope mounted on the barrel rather than the receiver. I've seen a few shotguns with barrel-mounted scopes, a la Jeff Cooper's Scout Rifle concept, but it's invariably a custom application.

A bolt-on scope mount is fine for turkey guns or short-range slug shooting but will move too much to provide accuracy at longer ranges.

Mounting the base directly on the receiver, or in this case, on the barrel of this H&R 980, is the best possible arrangement for accuracy. It is, however, rougher on the scope.

(I've never seen a commercial offering.) Shooting Times technical editor and fellow slug-hunting nut Dick Metcalf of Illinois has a barrel-mounted scope on his Remington 11-87 and I've got a custom 870 pump with a similar mount that came out of the now-defunct Slug Brothers shop in Ohio. I wouldn't want to enter one in a benchrest shooting competition, but you won't find a better point-and-shoot setup for hunting situations. Unfortunately, you aren't likely to find them on a dealer's shelf, either.

But there is an alternative. You can actually achieve roughly the same effect with a receiver-mounted, low-power scope by keeping both eyes open when aiming. My optometrist, who is also a hunter, suggested it long ago. And now, after dedicated practice, I am a true disciple of the two-eyes method. It takes a properly mounted (right height and eye relief) scope, but shooting with both eyes open gives you the optimum field of view, not to mention spatial awareness, that really comes in handy when shooting in the woods — and particularly at moving animals. When selecting a scope for a shotgun, whether it's a specialty shotgun scope or a good riflescope, I want more than 3 inches of eye relief; certainly nothing less than $3\,^1/_4$ inches. A good riflescope made to withstand heavy magnums (tested for .375 and higher) will usually have sufficient eye relief. That being said, I often opt for a good-quality riflescope to put on my slug guns because of the magnification.

One drawback to shotgun-only scopes is that they tend to be of low magnification with small objective lens. That means you lose precious minutes in low light conditions. Leupold, Nikon, Kahles and a few others do, however, offer two to seven variable shotgun scopes with larger objective lens and Sightron has a fixed 4-power with a large objective. I've got a 4x Leupold Compact through which I've viewed more deer than any other scope in my shop. The majority of shotgun scopes available today are variables that run from 1.5-2x to about 6-7x. Again, the size of the objective lens is critical for light transmission and field of view. Most high-end or upper mid-range riflescopes ($300 and up) are tested to withstand the recoil of a .375 magnum rifle and therefore should stand up to a shotgun's punishment. It won't be parallax-free at close range but that's a very minor factor that most shooters wouldn't even notice.

red-dot optics

Illuminated-dot electronic sighting devices – virtually standard in combat-style pistol competitions – have also found a home with slug and buckshot hunters, largely because they offer both long eye relief and a wide field of view. The Swedish-made Aimpoint celebrated its 25th anniversary at the turn of century, meaning that it was already well

is parallax important for slug shooting?

Does your scope have an adjustable objective? It's really the only way to eliminate parallax at long range. Parallax can account for a quarter- to a half-inch in a 100-yard rifle group, even though visual phenomenon is not nearly so critical with shotguns. What is parallax? "Parallax, in the sense of sports optics, is a visual distortion created when the image of the target is not focused on the same plane as the reticle," explains optics expert Dave Brown, national sales manager for Leica. "If both are focused on the same plane, there will be no change in the position of the reticle with respect to the target, no matter the position of the eye in relation as it looks through the scope. But if the target image is focused behind or in front of the reticle, the position of the reticle with respect to the target will shift as the eye is moved up and down or from side to side as it looks through the scope. Since it is virtually impossible to position the eye in exactly the same place for every shot, the condition of parallax can result in a loss of accuracy."

A simple way to demonstrate the effect of parallax is to hold up both thumbs, one at arm's length and one approximately 6 inches closer to the eye. Sight with one eye at the image of one thumb superimposed over the other. If you move your head, the position of the thumbs relative to each other will change. That's parallax. Now move the thumbs closer together so that they are touching, it eliminates the effect. A hardware example: You've got a scoped gun on a rest, the crosshairs centered on a bull's-eye 100 yards away. Looking through the scope at the target, if you move your head and established when it hit these shores as the first illuminated-dot sighting device in 1981. It is still the industry leader, even though virtually every other major optics manufacturer has a version of its own.

When buying an electronic dot sight, check to make sure that it is parallax-free, an important consideration. Most current models are pre-focused but parallax was an important check just a few years ago. That means if the scope and gun are stationary and you move your head, does the dot move on the target? If not, if the dot stays on the bull regardless of your head position, the scope is said to be parallax-free. Also consider that under some conditions, such as dim light (dusk or dawn) the dot, regardless of how low you adjust the illumination, will be so bright that it will darken the screen and keep you from aiming. Illuminated-dot sights are terrific against snowy backgrounds or in bright conditions.

Illuminated red-dot scopes are very popular with both slug and buckshot shooters due to their large field of view, long eye relief and point-and-shoot function.

the reticle moves in relation to the bull's-eye, that's parallax. If the reticle stays on the bull's-eye, regardless of where your eye moves, it's parallax-free. Shotgun scopes are usually focused to be parallax-free at 75 yards while riflescopes are typically focused at 150 yards.

Let's put that phenomenon in a scope tube. When light rays enter the tube through the curved objective (front) lens, they are bent inward so that they cross at some point. The crossing point is the point of focus. That point will move forward or backward as the distance to the target changes. If that focus point coincides with the position of the reticle, there is no parallax. If it does not, the effect will be much the same as the two thumbs held apart; the image of the reticle will shift with respect to the target as the position of the eye is changed. "In practical terms," Brown says, "parallax is not a significant issue in most shotgun hunting situations. If the shooter does experience parallax, the loss of accuracy at short range is so insignificant as to have virtually no effect in terms of shot placement. Under most hunting situations, there are other variables that probably have more impact on accuracy than parallax."

It's much different, however, for precision rifle shooting such as long-range targets or varmint shooting, where parallax can be a significant accuracy factor. This is why adjustable objectives are most often found on target and varmint scopes. The adjustable objective allows the shooter to manually focus the scope for the shooting range, so that the target image is always focused on the reticle plane, thereby eliminating parallax at all ranges.

adjusting the scope

It's truly amazing how many hunters don't know how to, or even that they should, focus their scope before using it. I'm talking about adjusting the ocular (rear) lens so that the reticle is clear before shooting. American-style scopes often feature an eyepiece threaded into the scope tube, held in place by a lock ring. To adjust them, loosen the lock ring and turn the eyepiece in or out until the crosshairs are sharply focused. It may take dozens of turns to achieve proper focus. This is not the case with European designs, which focus by turning the rear rim of the eyepiece to cam the ocular lens in or out. One turn is usually sufficient.

One tip: Do the focusing at dusk, when your eyes have their shallowest depth of field. You'll focus more precisely. Once the scope has been properly mounted, focused and bore-sighted, you should find that you are "on paper" at 25 yards. If you just mounted the scope, it may take a couple of shots for it to settle into the rings. Once it's settled, I make preliminary adjustments at 25 yards before fine-tuning at 50 and, under some circumstances, 100 yards. Remember that when using a scope you should move the reticle in the direction that you want the group to move. For example, if you are grouping left and below the bull's-eye, make the adjustment to the right and up.

Most high-quality scopes adjust at one-quarter inch per click at 100 yards. Click the knob four times and it will move the point of impact by an inch. That means if you are shooting at 50 yards it takes eight clicks to move the group by 1 inch; at 25 yards it will require 16 clicks. A common mistake made when zeroing a scope is to make your adjustments after taking only one shot. Always shoot a group, make the sight adjustment from the center of the group, and shoot a second group to determine if you are "zeroed." Often, especially with cheaper quality scopes, the adjustment won't register on the next shot and it may require two or three. The reason for this is that the adjustment spring in some scopes actually rides against the wall of the tube. When you make the adjustment by turning the turret, the spring may or may not wind properly if it is riding the wall. A shot or two will usually jostle it sufficiently for the adjustment to "take." That's the reason you might see folks make the adjustment then tap the scope tube a few times with a screwdriver or knife handle. But I'm real leery of hammering scope tubes, even if they don't belong to me.

Every major optics manufacturer now makes at least one model of scope specifically designed for shotguns.

range-finding scopes

Elsewhere in this book we explore the vagaries of wind deflection and the rainbow trajectory of shotgun slugs, situations that should point out the necessity of knowing the absolute yardage to your target. After botching shots on several deer over the years due to poor range "guesstimation," I now pack a laser rangefinder right along with my slug gun and ammunition. All are equally important in my book and it simply makes no sense to go hunting anymore without all three.

The Leica 1200 Scan is the best laser rangefinder I've ever used in hunting situations but the more affordable Bushnell and Nikon models which are identical except for product markings are perfectly suitable for ranging shotgun shots. Generally speaking, the higher the yardage rating on these instruments, the stronger the beam and the more efficient they will be in picking up questionable targets. Believe me, a buck that looks to be 60-70 yards away in a field can easily be 130 if there are a couple of unseen dips in the terrain between you and him. I can vouch for the fact that using a 70-yard sight picture for a 130-yard shot with a slug gun is likely to hurt your feelings more than it hurts the deer. Been there; done that – with witnesses. Similarly, it's very difficult to hold over in precisely the right position to hit a buck that's standing a measured 160 yards away in a cut field on a day with a slight crosswind. The latter condition, which I again have encountered, is the reason I now mount a range-finding scope on my slug guns if there is any chance of a long shot.

Top: If the receiver of your gun is too thin-walled to accept mount screws, use a cantilevered barrel to mount your scope.

Bottom: Saddle-style, bolt-on mounts are an improvement but are still impossible to keep totally stable, shot to shot.

At one time the sole province of snipers, range-finding scopes today readily find their way onto varmint and long-range competitors' rifles and more recently, slug guns. I mounted a 3-9x40 Burris FullField II Ballisti-Plex scope on my Tar-Hunt RSG-12 for a prairie hunt for pronghorns and buffalo a few years back and sighted it in so that the graduated crosshairs gave me dead-on aiming at 75, 120, 150 and 175 yards with Winchester Partition Gold slugs. No need for holdover or guesswork on the featureless, table-flat Wyoming prairie. The scope came with a pamphlet that gave graduations for various loads at various yardages but didn't include slugs. A simple range session on a calm day gave me just what I needed, however.

On a recent Texas whitetail hunt I fell in love with a Swarovski Habicht AV 4-12x50 scope with the ranging TDS Tri-Factor reticle system that I had mounted on a rifle. Unfortunately, I had to give it back, but I was sufficiently impressed to raid the cookie jar to get a more affordable

3-9 x 42mm Kahles (Swarovski sister company) American Hunter scope with the TDS system for my slug gun. It is simply the easiest-to-calculate, simplest-to-use, most-foolproof ranging scope system I've ever encountered. TDS is for designer Lt. Col. T.D. Smith, a former Air Force combat fighter pilot and Olympic and Pan-Am Games pistol shooter and team coach who licenses the system to Swarovski-Kahles.

A variation of a mil-dot scope, the TDS-Plex and TDS-4 reticles offer graduations for elevation and windage so that the shooter can hold dead-on the target from a variety of ranges under a variety of wind conditions. I've tried several mil-dot and range-finding scopes but found them too complicated or fragile for slug gun use. Not so the TDS system. The scope comes with a booklet to help calculate the scope's factor for a specific load and thus assign yardages to the various lateral marking bars. I ran into some initial problems putting slug statistics into the calculation system but the problems were quickly solved with a toll-free call to Swarovski Optik Customer Service. Later I found a bigger advantage in the easy-to-use (even I was able to operate it) Swarovski Ballistic Library CD that calculates each graduation and gives you more ballistic and trajectory information on specific loads than you'll ever need. Old-timers will likely snicker at the thought of a range-finding scope on a shotgun, but I'm not going hunting without it.

mounting
a shotgun scope

Even if your scope is the right style and magnification for your hunting or shooting needs, if it isn't mounted properly, it's worthless. And mounting a scope on a shotgun is a different proposition than putting one on your varmint rifle. Let's mount a shotgun scope the right way. Assuming that you've got the correct bases and rings (steel, not aluminum) for the scope, the first step should be to clean all of the screw holes of oil and debris as well as all of the contact surfaces, screws, rings and bases. I use an aerosol degreaser like Shooter's Choice Quick Scrub III, one that doesn't leave a film when it dries. Next — and I'm sure you've read this a thousand times before but it bears repeating — always use the right size and type of screwdriver or wrench. Screwdriver blades should be the correct thickness and the same width as the diameter of the screw and they should be hollow ground or parallel ground so that they fit snugly and don't slip.

Most screwdrivers you find at the local True Value will have tapered blades to "fit" more screws. Using them on a gun is asking for a distorted slot or marred finish on the gun, achieved when the damned blade slips out of the slot

Proper mounting of the scope is essential both for optimum accuracy and to avoid damage to the instrument.

to make a free bore "engraving" run of its own. If the screw is a Phillips-head, the suggestion is the same — make sure your screwdriver is the same size. Virtually all small Phillips screwdrivers will fit in all Phillips-head screws but, again, using the wrong size driver is asking for problems. Many scope-mounts today use Allen-head hex screws, which afford much better torque (more efficient tightening). They are a major improvement over slot and Phillips-head screws but they, too, must be matched with the right-sized wrench. Always use a wrench that is not only of the right size but one with clean, sharp edges that haven't been rounded by previous overzealous use and subsequent slippage. The line between "tight" and "stripped" is a fine one. I have converted virtually all of my base and ring screws to Torx heads, a unique six-pointed star-shape slot and attendant wrench that provides more gripping surface. That means more tightening power without stripping. Although it's not as much of a problem with shotguns as it is with rifles, you'll sometimes find that the various screws that come with

When fitting or adjusting a scope, always use the correct screwdriver blade or wrench to fit the screw.

what is eye relief?

Eye relief is the distance between your eye and the ocular lens of the scope when the full field of view is visible. Actually, that is optical eye relief. There is another form, practical eye relief, which is the measurement from the rim around the lens to your eye. The latter is the one that shotgun shooters should be most concerned with. Be advised that eye relief can change with the magnification in variable scopes. Most manufacturers will list eye relief in the specs for their scopes, but they won't tell you if that measurement is optical or practical. In my experience, most list optical eye relief, which may be as much as a half-inch longer than the more-telling practical version.

A shotgun requires more than 3 inches of eye relief to guard against denting the shooter's eyebrows.

Leupold scopes are legendary for excellent eye relief. To a slightly lesser extent, Swarovski-Kahles, Zeiss and Burris scopes generally offer sufficient eye relief for big-recoil guns. Recently I've been pleased with the eye relief of the Bushnell Elite 4200 series variable scopes. Be advised that there is a trade-off for long eye relief — a narrower field of view. If your shotgun has a typical shotgun stock (low comb designed to place the eye in line with the barrel rib), you'll have to raise your head slightly to see through any scope. This too makes it difficult to find the full field of view. Some specialty slug guns today offer Monte Carlo or at least rifle-like straight comb stocks suitable for scope-mounted guns, which not only makes scope use easier but also lessens felt recoil. My personal feeling is that field of view is overrated for hunting. Anyone used to handling a modern scoped firearm in hunting situations can easily find a deer in a 20-foot field of view just as easily as in a 30- or 40-foot field.

Never use the scope tube as a wrench ... I can't tell you the number of times I've seen tubes used as wrenches in this situation.

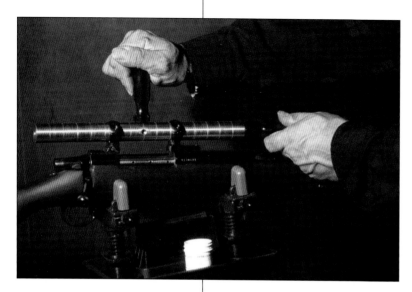

The author feels that lapping the rings of a shotgun scope is essential to the tight fit needed for the scope to withstand the recoil.

Proper alignment of the scope rings is essential to keep the mounts from torquing the scope tube.

Boresighting a scope saves a lot of time, aggravation and ammunition when sighting-in at the range.

bases are not all the same length. Make a "dry" run, running the screws into their respective holds and torquing them down to detemine if they are too long or two short.

Once you are sure you've got the right screws for the right holes, remove them and coat the screw threads and the contact surfaces of the base and the receiver with a locking adhesive like Loctite. Don't just put a drop in the screw hole as it may keep the screw from bottoming out. It is imperative to "dedicate" those screws to the receiver, given the magnum concussion that they will endure from slug or buckshot loads. Be advised that there are several strengths of Loctite. The super strength stuff can weld that sucker in place, never to separate. Maybe that's what you want, maybe not. I use lesser-strength Blue Loctite 242 on guns that come to me on loan or may need a base change at some point. If the bases are ever to be removed, heating the screwheads with a soldering gun should break the hold. If you are using adjustable rings (Millett, Weaver, Burris, et al.), the bottom rings should then be loosely fastened to the base and aligned using a 1-inch diameter hardwood or aluminum dowel 12 inches long. Placing the dowel in the rings, check for lateral variation and adjust.

I like to use a Brownell's alignment kit, which consists of two pointed aluminum bars. Install a bar in each ring, with the pointed ends facing each other, and align the rings (using alternating screw tension) until the points line up perfectly. If you are using Leupold, Burris or Ruger-style rings that are turned into the base for perfect alignment, use a specialty wrench, aluminum rod or hardwood dowel in the rings to torque them into place. Never use the scope tube. As obvious as that sounds, I can't tell you the number of times I've seen tubes used as wrenches in this situation. I am in the process of changing all of my bases and rings to the rugged Warne design. Warne rings are solid, square-edged, machined steel that virtually align themselves upon mounting and resist recoil like no other system I've found.

Next — and this is important for scope mounting on heavy recoiling guns — lap the inside saddles of the rings (top and bottom) with a piece of 320-grit wet-dry sandpaper wrapped around the dowel. I use a lapping bar instead of the dowel to both align the rings and administer the lapping process with compound. This will smooth the mounting surface to assure a larger bearing surface and reduce marring of the scope tube when inserted. Lap until you've achieved about 80 percent bearing surface on the rings. If you go much more it may actually make the tube a loose fit in the rings. I like to add a dab of rubber cement inside the

lapped rings before mounting the scope to further guard against movement. Before I lay the scope in the rings, I like to center the crosshairs so that I'll have the best possible range of adjustment later. To do this I turn each adjustment dial until it stops, then turn it the other way counting the clicks until it stops again. Then turn it back half the number of clicks and it's centered. Now lay the scope in the rings, tightening the screws snug enough to hold it but not so tight that you can't move the tube in the rings. Tighten screws alternately, first left rear, then right front, then right rear, etc., turning them the same amount each time to keep the gap between the top and bottom rings equal.

This systematic rotation of screw tightening not only minimizes the stress on the scope tube but also keeps it square with the barrel. Turning one more than another will torque the tube in the rings. Don't bottom the screws just yet. Leave the scope somewhat loose so that you can adjust for eye relief (at least 3 inches from scope to brow) and crosshair alignment. You should slide the scope forward and back with your head in aiming position, cheek to stock, seeking a bright, complete field of view that is a complete circle. Also adjust the eyepiece so that the crosshairs are totally clear. At this point you should also align the crosshairs. Everyone looks through a scope with a little different head position, which is why the crosshairs don't look vertical when you look through your buddy's scope.

The author uses this reticle-leveling device to make sure that the crosshairs are absolutely vertical and horizontal – a big factor in long-range accuracy.

If you're going to adjust your view through the scope, do it with perfectly aligned crosshairs absolutely vertical and horizontal. For an exact alignment, I like to use a simple gadget called a reticle leveler, which saddles over the scope tube and is held in place by rubber bands. Perfect alignment of the crosshairs is essential to long-range accuracy. Once the eye relief is correct and the crosshairs are aligned, tighten the ring screws, again alternating a slight tightening of first one, then the other until both are torqued down well. Again, you can tell on many adjustable two-piece rings if the pressure is even by comparing the gap in the mating of the top and bottom rings at the side. This is not necessary with Warne, Leupold, Burris or Ruger-style rings, which actually cam into alignment when seated.

Next, if you have a collimator (boresighter), align the scope and bore. If you don't have one, look down the bore to the target and zero the scope to the same target. There are also a variety of laser bore-alignment tools that work well in place of a mechanical boresighter, but many need as much as 25 feet of space ahead of the barrel to operate. If the scope won't "zero" within the limitations of the adjusting turrets, you'll have to pull the whole system apart, place a shim in one or the other rings, reassemble and try again. A shim – I cut up aluminum beverage cans since their wall thickness is about 0.002 of an inch – can move the scope's point of aim by an inch at 100 yards. After the appropriate adjustments are made, the scope should be aligned close enough to print on a target at 25 yards. Make any individual adjustments at that range until the scope is absolutely zeroed, then make further adjustments at 50.

Shotguns for Big Game

on the western plains

"The buck on the left is 191 yards," said outfitter-guide Scott Denny, peering through a laser rangefinder at a group of bedded pronghorns on the high plains (elevation 4,800 feet) of east-central Wyoming. "We can get closer if we stay behind this little ridge to the right." "No. I'll try it from here," said hunter Steve Meyer, readying his gun on a bi-pod for the shot. "How hard do you think that wind is?" "I dunno. Ten [mph], maybe a little more," said Denny, switching from rangefinder to binoculars. Meyer carefully lined up the crosshairs, shifted them for windage, and slowly exhaled while he pressed the trigger. "Boom!" At the report the herd leapt to its collective feet and after the first couple of strides, the animals were running flat-out in the unique gliding gait indigenous to the species. All of them were obviously very intent on getting somewhere else very quickly. All but one, the targeted buck never got out of his bed and was now lying in a twisted pile with one leg in the air.

It was a nice shot — for a shotgun. Meyer was shooting a 12-gauge Browning A-Bolt. The projectile was one of Winchester's Partition Gold slugs. Posessing well over 1,800 feet per second of muzzle velocity, more than one and a half tons of energy at the muzzle and a projectile comprised of a lead core with a partitioned copper jacket, the Partition Gold is only technically a shotgun slug. Sighted-in to be dead-on at 150 yards, the slug offered a point-blank range *(plus or minus 3 inches of elevation, assuring no need of holdover)* of 178 yards. Meyer, who had been a member of the slug's design team at Winchester-Olin, gave 2 inches of holdover at 191 yards and allowed for about 6 inches of wind drift.

"Shotguns?" had been Denny's surprised reaction the day before when Meyer uncased his A-Bolt and I pulled out my Tar-Hunt RSG-12 custom bolt gun. But after watching us both shoot rifle-like 100-yard groups from a makeshift bench at the Table Mountain Outfitters tent camp outside the tiny prairie town of Shawnee (pop. 8. Yeah, 8), he was a convert. Denny was also at my shoulder that first day when I took a pronghorn buck with an offhand shot of 117 yards in a milling herd that we surprised by popping up from a dry ravine bed. "I was impressed," said Denny, whose Table Mountain Outfitters also put on whitetail and mule deer, mountain lion, turkeys, upland birds and

Next page:
Illinois hunter Steve Meyer took this Wyoming pronghorn at 191 yards with a Winchester Partition Gold slug fired from a Browning A-Bolt shotgun.

buffalo hunts in Nebraska and South Dakota. "I wasn't so sure at first but after seeing those things in action I figure that's all you need anywhere they're legal."

Triple U ranch hand Clint Amiotte was similarly skeptical a few days later when we showed up equipped with shotguns to take a buffalo from the Triple U Ranch's herd located near Fort Pierre, South Dakota. Admittedly, shooting a buffalo shouldn't be confused with hunting, but then it never could. The American bison is horribly myopic and decidedly indifferent to intruders when they approach from downwind. Hunting bison is much the same today as it was 130 years ago when market hunters reduced the herds from an estimated 30 million to near-extinction. Bison may not be wary, but they are extremely tough animals. The typical $6\frac{1}{2}$-year-old bull weighs between 1,800 and 1,900 pounds with massive, heavily furred shoulders and neck and large bone structure. Amiotte was skeptical that a shotgun slug could effectively work its way through the heavy hide, let alone the muscle and bone.

Using the rolling topography of the 62,000-acre Triple U Ranch (where much of the movie *Dances with Wolves* was filmed), we were

The author took this 1,850-pound plains bison in South Dakota with a Winchester Partition Gold slug and his Tar-Hunt slug gun.

able to slip within 90 yards of a small group of bulls standing separated from a herd of about 500 animals. Bavarian Eric Fischer, a fellow Table Mountain hunter who traveled with us to the Triple U, borrowed my Tar-Hunt slug gun and felled the first bull with a single well-placed shot to the neck. "Whoa!" yelled Amiotte, who had seen hundreds of buffalo shot on the ranch — but none with a shotgun. "That shotgun slug is a real slobber-knocker ain't it?" Well, that's one word for it. My bull took two shots; the first was a quartering-to shot to the shoulder on a walking animal at slightly more than 100 yards. I was then able to move around the hobbled bull and the "slobberknock-er" put him down with a 90-yard neck shot.

The Partition Gold is part of a vanguard of impressive new loads that have been pushing the envelope in shotgun slug performance. The new loads have been described as rifle fod-der disguised as shotgun slugs. Despite its flashy ballistics and design, the Winchester load isn't even the fastest or hard-hitting on the market right now. "Some say that the fast slugs need a faster twist rate but I think interior barrel diameter is more of a factor," said Randy Fritz, owner of Tar-Hunt Custom Guns and research and development coordinator for Lightfield. "I think you're going to find that most guns made in the last three years will shoot them fine but anything made before that might or might not handle them well. That's because in 1997 SAAMI (Shooting Arms and Ammunition Manufacturers Institute) instituted a standard bore size for 12-gauge rifled barrels (minimum .719, plus .003) and the newer guns will have standardized barrels where as earlier guns may be virtually any size." The bison and pronghorn hunts were, admittedly, done as demonstrations of modern slug performance. No one would purposely pursue those animals with a shotgun when rifles are perfectly legal. But shotguns and slugs are very common ordnance for some other big game. I've taken several black bears over bait, several wild hogs and four caribou with shotguns and slugs and I'm planning a trip to northern Ontario for muskox and another to South Africa for plains game and birds using only Ithaca shotguns. The technology of slug per-formance and improvements in slug-shooting shotguns have taken giant strides forward and today's hunters are reaping the benefit.

Top: The author had to battle with both distance and the wind to take this Wyoming pronghorn with a Winchester Partition Gold slug.

Bottom: The author has taken several bears over bait with a shotgun. This 6-foot Manitoba black bear fell to a Remington Copper Solid.

Gun Care
cleaning a slug gun

Everyone knows that shotguns used to hunt deer should be cleaned regularly. Of course, everyone also knows the virtue of low-fat foods, well-fitting shoes, flossing and safe sex, but how many of us pay attention to them? Actually, the benefit of cleaning guns is more likely to be observed because it's a seasonal rite of sorts; something passed down from father to son for generations. It was, in fact, a ritual in our family to sight-in our slug guns prior to the season, then clean the bores to a bright sheen before storing them for opening day. Little did we realize that our unquestioning respect for shotgun bore hygiene was actually destroying the potential accuracy of our first shot with a slug.

Experienced shooters by now probably know that smoothbore barrels often need some lead fouling to shrink the barrel's internal diameter sufficiently to "hug" full-bore slugs and throw them accurately. Get the barrel squeaky clean and you'll shoot patterns rather than groups for a while. It's different, however, if you use a rifled bore and sabot slugs. Since the sabot slug never touches the barrel, there is no lead residue to foul the barrel. Conventional velocity sabot slugs will deposit only a small amount of fouling – actually graphite that works like moly-coating – and little else in the wake of each shot. The higher-velocity slugs tend to leave a bit more plastic fouling since the sabots are subjected to much higher pressure, and that can affect accuracy after dozens of shots.

If you have a ported barrel, however, sabot fouling can become a problem. The sharp edges of the ports shave small amounts of material from the polyethylene sabot sleeves as they pass through and plastic residue tends to accumulate on the edges of the holes. Since the fouling builds up unevenly, it tends to influence subsequent rounds. The ports should be scrubbed regularly. The buildup may not seem significant but I've seen several good-shooting slug guns, including one of Randy Fritz's custom Tar-Hunts, that lost quite a bit of accuracy, but recovered immediately when the ports were cleaned.

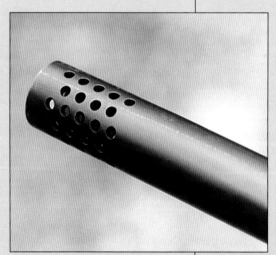

Above: The ports on a shotgun bore need to be cleaned regularly and totally since the plastic buildup from shotcups or sabots will quickly affect buckshot patterning or slug accuracy.

Next page:
Rifled bores that shoot sabot slugs do not need cleaning very often since the slug never touches the barrel and sabots don't leave a wash like conventional shotgun wads. The exception is high-velocity sabot loads, which do leave residue from the sabots.

cleaning up after buckshot

Above: A non-marring shotgun cleaning rod can be fashioned from a wooden dowel and bicycle handle.

Right: Buckshot shooters should use a brush to clean the choke tube or choke area of the muzzle. Slug shooters can use the same brush to clean ported muzzles.

Below: Cleaning your gun after shooting is like doing dishes after a good meal — it's not the part you look forward too, but it's necessary.

Buckshot loads are another exception to the "don't-clean-it" concept since lead loads without shotcups leave metal fouling in the barrel and those with shotcups can leave a substantial plastic wash as well as powder fouling. Powder and plastic wad fouling reach a point where they place drag on subsequent shotcups and pull them away from loads, thus negating their controlling and containing functions.

Riflemen are warned to stay away from hardened or stainless steel jointed rods since they can scratch a bore or mar rifling. Since the steel in shotgun barrels is even softer than rifle steel, it makes sense to avoid the same thing. Jointed aluminum rods are similarly unhealthy since a soft metal like aluminum can pick up grit and act just like a lap, scratching the lands and grooves of a rifled barrel or the mirror finish of a shotgun tube. I use nylon-coated rods from Dewey or Bore Tech. For cleaning 12-gauge shotguns, an excellent patch rod can be made from a 5/8-inch wooden dowel with a plastic bicycle handle-bar grip fastened to one end.

An absorbent paper towel *(we've found Bounty brand works best)* folded and rolled to bore-filling diameter is an excellent shotgun-cleaning patch. Soak the towel with bore solvent and push it through the length of the bore from chamber to muzzle. Continue to wet brush and wet patch until the bore is clean. If you want to remove plastic wad or sabot fouling, use a little common sense and don't buy any solvent that comes in a plastic bottle. If it doesn't eat through a plastic container, it won't melt away plastic wad fouling.

Use only phosphorus bronze brushes wound on a core for shotguns or rifles. Stainless steel brushes are so hard they will score some shotgun barrel steel. Always use a rest to hold the firearm steady while working the cleaning rod. The rest should have padding and should be built so that the muzzle is lower than the receiver so that solvents drain away from the chamber and stock wood. If I'm going to store the gun for a while, I might run a wet patch through the barrel to leave a protective film but always swab it out before shooting again.

cleaning choke tubes

Screw-in choke tubes also require special attention. If they are ported, they will definitely need to be scrubbed regularly with a choke tube cleaner like Shooter's Choice to get rid of wad or sabot fouling scraped off by the ports. Even non-ported tubes need extra scrubbing since they catch the full brunt of a slug being slammed into it at peak velocity, which is bound to shave and shape that slug. I keep a stainless steel barrel tank filled with solvent year-around and soak my trap and occasionally slug gun barrels in it before giving them a thorough cleaning. I realize that a couple of gallons of bore solvent is a pretty dear investment.

A trapshooting friend makes an affordable and suitable alternative by mixing equal parts of kerosene, paint thinner, Dextron III automatic transmission fluid and Acetone. See the sidebar on the mixture known as Ed's Red Bore Cleaner *(page 104)*. Similarly I use a special chamber brush to clean that area, which is prone to carbon buildup. I mentioned a quick field cleaning after each shooting session. Remember that the rods should always be wiped clean and the brushes should have the solvent rinsed out of them with a degreasing agent. Solvent is meant to dissolve gilded metal and doesn't know the difference between residue and a bronze or brass bristles. Use a toothbrush to scrub bearing surfaces with bore solvent to clean actions. Then wipe it off, spray with a degreaser and coat the metal surfaces (including the inside of the tube) with a quality moisture displacer.

Lubrication is often overrated and in many cases can be more of a detriment than an advantage. A small amount of lubricant may help when breaking in a new gun to ease the wear in metal-on-metal contact areas, but most folks use too much. Excess lubricant can gum up the action by attracting grime or actually impeding the action when it changes consistency in extreme conditions. If a grease is rated for extreme temperatures, its label will likely proudly proclaim the fact. If not, beware. I use Shooter's Choice high-temperature grease that is tested to retain its viscosity in baking oven temperatures or cold too severe for humans to endure. When using a grease or oil lubricant, the rule of thumb is "if you can see it, it's too much." Use sparingly and always check the temperature range on the product label. If the range isn't listed, chances are you're holding something that turns into gunk in extreme cold weather. If you're concerned with slug accuracy, buckshot patterning, durability or future convenience, the bottom line is that a little tender loving care never hurt any relationship.

When buying a lubricant, check its temperature range. Shotguns, especially autoloaders, have been known to "gum up" in extreme cold conditions when the lubricants solidified.

storing your guns

A gun exposed to the elements, or one brought in from extreme cold into a warmed environment, will likely be wet and water is an obvious enemy when it is allowed to sit on metal. In those situations all guns should obviously be wiped down thoroughly with a dry cloth; disassembled to get at ambient moisture in the interior; then sprayed liberally with a moisture-displacing agent such as Shooter's Choice Rust Prevent. Apply one coat, let it set 30 seconds and wipe it off — then spray again with a lighter coat before putting the gun away in its case or vault.

homemade bore cleaner: ed's red

Competitive shooters have a history of concocting a variety of witches brews as homemade alternatives to high-priced commercial bore cleaning products. One of the most effective homemade bore solvent/cleaning agents I've ever encountered is one adapted from an old Frankford Arsenal recipe by well-known industry figure Ed Harris, who worked with both Ruger and the military. A shooting buddy showed me a piece that Harris wrote on "Ed's Red" Bore Cleaner in the mid-1990s and I keep a bath of the stuff in a covered stainless steel barrel soaking tray year-around. A word of caution: This stuff is caustic and flammable and should only be used out-side or in a well-ventilated area, a description that certainly defines my breezy backyard workshop. Precautions should be taken and directions should be followed exactly. When mixed and used correctly, this stuff is really, really effective at dissolving carbon residue, cleansing the barrel and protecting the steel finish against corrosion, and it costs a fraction of the price of most commercial bore solvents.

Harris' recipe is based on proven principles and incorporates two polar and two non-polar ingredients. It is adapted from a formula in *Hatcher's Notebook* for "Frankford Arsenal Cleaner No.18" by substituting equivalent modern ingredients. The original Hatcher recipe called for equal parts of acetone, turpentine, Pratts Astral Oil and sperm oil, and optionally 200 grams of lanolin added per liter. Harris found that Pratts Astral Oil turned out to be nothing more than acid-free deodorized kerosene. We substituted K-1 kerosene of the type normally sold for indoor space heaters. An inexpensive, effective substitute for sperm oil is Dextron (II, IIe or III) automatic transmission fluid (ATF). The additives in automatic transmission fluid that include organometallic antioxidants and surfactants make it highly suitable for our intended purpose.

Hatcher's original formula used gum spirits of turpentine, but tur-pentine is expensive and highly flammable. Cheaper and safer is aliphat-ic mineral spirits, which is a petroleum based "safety solvent" used for thinning oil-based paints and as automotive parts cleaner. It is common-ly sold under the names "odorless mineral spirits," "Stoddard Solvent" or "Varsol." The lanolin is optional and Ed's Red works well without it. Incorporating the lanolin makes the cleaner easier on the hands, and pro-vides better residual lubrication and corrosion protection if you use the cleaner as a protectant for long-term storage. If you want to minimize cost, you can leave the lanolin out and save about $8 per gallon.

As noted previously, run a solvent-soaked patch or one soaked with Rust Prevent down a clean barrel before storing the gun. Be sure to swab the barrel to remove any residue before using it again. I keep fresh silica bags in my gun vaults to discourage rusting and keep a vigilant eye on the moisture monitoring strips to know when to replace the bags.

Ingredients: One part Dextron II, IIe or III ATF, GM Spec. D-20265 or later. One part kerosene — deodorized, K1. One part Aliphatic Mineral Spirits, Fed. Spec. TT-T-2981F, CAS #64741-49-9, or substitute "Stoddard Solvent," CAS #8052-41-3, or equivalent, (aka "Varsol") and one part Acetone, CAS #67-64-1. An optional ingredient is one pound of lanolin, anhydrous, USP per gallon, OK to substitute lanolin, modified, topical lubricant, from the drug store.

Mixing instructions: Mix outdoors, in good ventilation. Use a clean 1-gallon chemical-resistant metal or plastic container — heavy-gage PET (polyethylene terephthalate) or PVC (Poly Vinyl Chloride). NFPA approved plastic gasoline storage containers are also OK. Do NOT use HDPE (High-density polyethylene), which is breathable because the acetone will evaporate. The acetone in Ed's Red will attack HDPE after about six months, making a heck of a mess.

Add the ATF first. Use the empty container to measure the other components, so that it is thoroughly rinsed. If you incorporate the lanolin into the mixture, melt it carefully in a double boiler, taking precautions against fire. Pour the melted lanolin into a larger container, rinsing the lanolin container with the bore cleaner mix, and stirring until it is all dissolved. Harris recommended diverting a small quantity, up to 4 ounces per quart, of the 50-50 ATF/kerosene mix for use as an "Ed's Red-compatible" gun oil. This can be safely done without impairing the effectiveness of the final mix.

I soak my shotgun barrels in a bath of Ed's Red for a couple of days, then work a bore brush through the barrel, scrubbing in 4- to 5-inch repeated strokes, to remove stubborn residue. Then I run a couple of wet patches through, then dry ones until they come out clean. If you are using Ed's Red as a solvent on a patch, leaving it to soak for at least a minute after applying it will improve its function. Harris said that leaving the bore wet will protect it from rust for up to 30 days and that if the lanolin is incorporated into the mixture, it will protect the firearm from rust for up to two years. Always wipe Ed's Red from exterior surfaces before storing the gun. While Ed's Red is said to be harmless to blued and nickel metal finishes, the acetone will attack most wood finishes. I also like to run a couple of dry patches through the bore before shooting again. Again, it's flammable, caustic and should only be used and stored in areas with adequate ventilation.

The Lightfield Hybred and a well-maintained slug gun proved effective on this Wyoming pronghorn at 122 yards.

Common sense dictates that all guns should be stored in a manner that discourages access by unwanted hands. Hanging on the den wall or in a windowed case is a decorative use for a firearm, but not a wise one. I grew up in a time when you could always find a gun behind the kitchen door, in the mudroom or barn of a rural home, back when members of the school shooting team carried rifles on the school bus with them. There was far more access to firearms back then, but far fewer problems with gun violence or misuse. The difference, if you'll allow me a second on the soapbox, was respect. As kids we knew that handling a gun was a privilege to be earned. It's not like that today and gun owners have a responsibility to keep firearms out of the hands of the careless, devious, ignorant or disrespectful.

Chris Young and his wife Emma with Pennsylvania bucks taken with their Collet Cup slugs. Chris used a 20-gauge, 250-grain slug while Emma's deer fell to a 300-grain 12-gauge version.

Certainly a build-the-house-around-it, thick-walled, 100 percent fireproof, bank-certified locking system gun vault would be the ideal for both security and protection of the guns, but it's overkill for folks like me and prohibitive for most of the rest of us. The choice of a storage container is a personal one. Are your guns utilitarian and you simply want to keep unauthorized hands off them or do they have financial and/or sentimental value and thus need to be protected from theft or damage? The answer should dictate what type of storage container you need. In my case, I own a lot of guns and usually have several others in my shop on loan from manufacturers for testing purposes. But I don't own or possess any truly valuable (four-figure price tag) guns and my shop has fire-resistant $5/8$-inch Sheetrock™ walls and a dead-bolt door lock.

The guns are reasonably protected against fire and outside elements and casual intruders. The main concern is keeping folks who do gain entrance to the shop from handling the guns without permission. Thus, two inexpensive keyed steel gun cabinets bolted to the floor and wall are all I need. In my upstairs gun room-office, however, which is more accessible and less resistant to fire, I have a Sentry 14-gun safe. The 375-pound safe features much thicker walls, five-dead bolt lock-up to discourage anyone short of a torch-wielding professional. Again, the guns aren't spectacularly valuable so a $3,000 half-ton fireproof vault isn't necessary. The $600 Sentry safe with a wheeled combination lock provides all the security needed.

Handloading for Shotguns

why handload?

Frankly, handloading accurate, hard-hitting shotgun slugs or good-patterning buckshot loads is pretty much beyond the capabilities of most of us. And it's viewed as largely unnecessary, given the accuracy and energy of most commercially loaded slugs and buckshot loads today. But there are some innovative tinkerers out there who have developed some pretty impressive loads, often operating well beyond the parameters that define the boundaries of commercial ammunition performance.

These are guys who are never satisfied with commercial products, and while they bristle at the price of high-tech slug or buckshot loads, the real reason they handload is to improve on what's available or provide something that isn't. You can't find, for instance, 28-gauge slugs or 10-gauge sabots, or hard-hitting .410 loads but you can handload some. These guys have developed some pretty impressive loads that often operate well beyond the parameters of commercial ammunition performance.

A friend of mine, for instance, has developed a special slug load that he uses to hunt elk that retains more energy at 100 yards than a .30-06, 180-grain cartridge produces at the muzzle! It's a one-off load, since the hull is pretty much ruined after one use. Furthermore, it can only be shot in a custom gun such as the Tar-Hunt, which is massively overbuilt to withstand high chamber pressures that would rupture any commercial shotgun on the market. I've seen some absolutely awesome accuracy achieved using handloaded target loads, as well. The advantage of handloading, if you are knowledgeable, is that loads can be tailored to an individual gun. Improving on commercial load energy, however, will be difficult without raising the chamber pressure to dangerous levels.

Lyman makes this popular sabot type slug for handloaders.

Next page:
Handloading slugs on a progressive press can be difficult, as there are usually stages that have to be manipulated by hand.

another dimension to shooting

Regardless of your reasoning, handloading definitely adds another dimension to shooting. There is a remarkable added feeling of satisfaction when one takes a deer with a slug or load that he loaded himself. By personally handling all of the components that collectively make up a given load, a shooter is more in touch with the requirements of the shooting conditions. Just taking a box of shells off a dealer's shelf keeps pellet or slug sizes, powder charges and their applications abstract. Studying the various sizes and parts of a shotshell and considering the conditions under which they will be used connects the shooter with all of the elements of shooting. That's what got me into reloading – the desire to plan, handle and assemble each load and the subsequent sense of pride and accomplishment when that load performs well. It's the same reason a woman knits a sweater or crafts a quilt when good-quality commercial variations are available; the same reason people build their own cabins or boats rather than contracting to have it done. It's the same reason, come to think of it, that I hunt rather than accept my meat butchered and served up between Styrofoam and cellophane.

loading for economy

Another of the many reasons to handload shotshells is, of course, economy. If you are going to shoot a substantial number of, say, saboted slugs or Hevi-Shot buckshot loads, handloads will likely cost less than a third the cost of what factory shells cost. The next most popular reason, I would guess, would be the ability to tailor a load to your wants and needs. Customizing ammunition to reduce velocity levels for lower recoil or adjust shot size and charge weights for specific purpose and performance are advantages afforded the reloader.

Unlike metallic cartridge reloading, each shotshell load carries with it specific and absolute components that must be used. If you can get a good buy on Brand A wads as opposed to the specified Brand B, you can't use them unless you find a load specifying Brand A – regardless of what the well-meaning but under-informed salesclerk says about interchangeability of components. If you are bargain hunting, take along a reloading manual to determine if data exists for the components you want to buy.

GUALANDI   LYMAN

handloading slug tips

Handloading slugs with a rolled crimp which, again, is the most efficient performance-wise but the biggest pain in the butt loading-wise is essentially a one-at-a-time proposition. The roll crimp is preferred for slug loads because of the uneven crimping surface provided by the nose of the slug. For roll crimping, the hull must be secured in a Hull Vise and wad pressure set at 40 pound to ensure proper wad seating and the evacuation of air between the powder and the wad. In most cases the wads were partially sealed into the hull, then the slug was inserted into the sabot, followed by the 40-pounds seating process and completed by crimping. Roll crimping requires a smooth hull mouth and, as noted previously, you aren't going to get that with a folded crimp hull.

The Hull Vise and hull should be positioned on a drill press table and the roll crimp starter (inserted in the drill chuck) slowly lowered into the mouth of the hull. The friction generated from the spinning tool will soften the crimp. Too slow a speed or too fast will likely screw up the process; they say that 300 rpm is ideal but how do you measure that? With a little practice you'll discern the right speed and the correct amount of down pressure. You can use 3-inch fold-crimped hulls as 2 $^3/_4$-inch slug hulls for roll crimping by trimming a quarter-inch at the bottom of the fold crimp. It's still much better, however, to use roll-crimped production slug hulls to make roll-crimped handloads.

Slug hulls are shorter than the shotshell variety since the shorter crimp makes it easier to get the slug out of the hull efficiently. You'll also find that if you use other star-crimped hulls and cut them for roll crimping, you'll never get good performance from that hull. Good hulls can easily be reloaded five or six times, sometimes as many as 10 times if the loads are not too severe. In fact, we've seen the performance of handloads that used commercial slug hulls get demonstrably better after two or three loadings of a particular hull sometimes dropping the standard deviation to less than 5 feet per second. In effect, the plastic in the hulls are losing resiliency and are conforming to the specific dimensions of that shotgun chamber. In effect, they are fire-formed like rifle brass, which expands to precisely fit a particular gun's chamber. I suspect that another factor of the repeated firings has more import than chamber fit. The slug's crimp is critical to performance and after a couple of loadings and firings the crimp fold will lose its stiffness and open with less resistance upon ignition – sort of like breaking in a new pair of shoes.

There is obviously a limit to the life of a reloading hull and each should be inspected closely after each firing. Check for interior damage from the powder burn and exterior flaws made by an ejector arm or maybe being crushed underfoot. Also check the base wad. It should be there, obviously, tight and not missing any chunks. Hull shape-up tools are great for inserting and working around the crimp area, relaxing the folds and giving you or the loader more room to work with.

Handloading buckshot allows the shooter to tailor the load to his gun and will generally be cheaper than buying commercial loads. .

follow the recipe exactly

Remember that every load takes a specific primer. Substituting one primer for another can diminish or exaggerate performance and almost certainly will alter interior ballistics, which ain't good. Powders are tailored to load objectives. Slug weight, velocity goals and expected air temperatures are factors when selecting a powder. Cold-temperature slugs and lighter slugs will require faster-burning powders for consistent burns. Use a slow-burning powder to tweak a light slug to high velocity only when the conditions are acceptable. Sealing wads will differ with the various slugs and powder combinations. In many cases conventional cushioned shotcup wads came to be used as sabots for rifled barrel loads. Whatever wad you use must seal the gases behind the slug in order to provide consistency. If you're using a fold crimp, it must be pushed open from the exact center or the slug will enter the barrel tilted. Depending on the style of the slug, it may be difficult to align the nose perfectly every time; that is why overshot wads are needed. It brings the point of force off the outside edge rather than the slug nose.

Some loads, particularly those loaded for smoothbores, require Teflon wrappers to be wrapped around the slug to make the projectile conform more tightly to the barrel. They seem to improve accuracy and reduce deformation of the slug. Always take into consideration the air temperature when you will be shooting the slugs. Powder loses energy,as the air gets colder. All lose a percentage but not at a fixed variable. Each powder type and burn rate is different. If you are loading at 70 degrees but are looking for performance at 30 degrees, it obviously must be loaded slightly hotter. Fast-burning powders lose less energy with falling temperatures; slow-burning powders lose more, probably because the pressure curve is spread out more and the energy is delivered over a longer period of time. If that pressure is not maintained, due to energy loss during cold temperatures, the burning cycle is hampered and consistency and energy are lost. Low chamber pressure and an ungodly amount of free bore make consistent slug accuracy problematical. When you think about it, you have to wonder why today's slugs shoot as well as they do.

Consider the chamber fit. A 2 3/4-inch slug actually unfolds to about 2 5/8 inches. In a 3-inch chamber, which is what you find in 99 percent of all commercial slug guns, that means a 3/8-inch jump from the .809-inch diameter chamber to the throat of the .729-diameter (.718 in a rifled bore) barrel. If you have a 3 1/2-inch chamber, that's 7/8 of an inch of freebore! Imagine that scenario in a rifle. That's the case with Foster-style or short slugs. Actually the rear of sabot and attached-wad slugs is still in the hull or very shortly removed from same, which means it's evenly supported when the nose of the slug reaches the throat of a 3-inch chamber, but in a 3 1/2-inch chamber it's pretty much a leap of faith. In fact, Lightfield suggests against shooting its 2 3/4-inch Hybred sabots in 3 1/2-inch chambers (*only selected Mossberg models offer rifled barrels with that size*

Sabot Specialties HammerHead slug is popular with handloaders since the one-piece sabot can be fitted with a variety of projectiles.

chambers) for fear that the thin-walled sabot halves will be dislodged from the slug while it traverses the freebore and will be jammed back together when the projectile hits the throat. Although the scenario has never caused any catastrophes, it certainly can cause a pressure spike and, at the very least, a healthy jolt of recoil.

handloading equipment

Your biggest cash outlay will be the purchase of reloading equipment, but that cost can be amortized over years of shooting. If you just want to try shotshell reloading to see if you like it, many metallic cartridge-reloading presses can be fitted to load shotshells. Actually you can get a shotgun-specific loader for about $50 that is an excellent beginning tool. Although I don't use it for loading slugs, a good progressive press like my RCBS Grand can last a lifetime and that's what I'm expecting. I use the Grand year-around for reloading trap and skeet loads. It mounts easily on the edge of a bench and is by far the most efficient and clean-loading press I've ever used, which makes it much easier to visualize as a lifetime partner. Let's understand right up front that reloading is not for everyone. If you must smoke, have distractions nearby, are naturally careless or daring – or if you're the type who doesn't read directions until after you get into trouble – you are much better off purchasing your ammo at WalMart. A mature, sensible approach is essential. If you understand and have no problem with the fact that components are not interchangeable and that the reloading process must be conducted with extreme care, thought and precision, you are a candidate for reloading.

the loading process

The actual process of loading shotshells, including buckshot, is pretty straightforward. What follows is the step-by-step process on a nonprogressive press, the simplest available. This type of press loads one shell at a time, the shell manually moved form die station to die station until all the operations have been performed.

The case body and metal head is full-length resized; the fired primer removed (decapping); a new primer seated (priming); the powder charge dropped; the wad seated; shot charge dropped (slugs have to be hand-inserted); the crimp started and the final crimp applied. You may want to use a specialized roll-crimper for slugs. While there may be minor operational differences among presses, they are likely minor and will be covered in the instructional manual that comes with each press. Progressive presses perform all of the same functions, in the same relative order, as those outlined in the preceding paragraphs, but the functions are performed on each pull of the lever at different stations on different hulls.

The loading process in a progressive press starts with the tool shell plate empty. You insert a case, perform the first step, advance the shell plate, insert a second case, perform two operations, and so on, until the press has six cases in the shell plate — one positioned at each station. After that you will need to simply keep feeding cases and components in order to obtain a fully loaded round for each down-up stroke of the press handle. The loading process begins at the left front of the tool, progresses counterclockwise, and the finished round is removed from the 9 o'clock position. Even modest efforts on most nonprogressive presses will yield the reloader 100 or more buckshot rounds per hour although it's a much slower proposition with slugs.

fodder for handloaders

I only wish I'd collected all the various slug designs that have crossed this desk over the years. There have been some really bizarre designs and some that were brutally functional. Many never got off the ground or took off and crashed landed due to logistics, poor planning or bad business partners. I don't think I'll ever forget Floridian Bill Wosenitz who pioneered the Venturi Helix projectile design for handloaders. The unique concept of a tubular helix slug and nylon "pusher" plug started out on the drawing board as a pistol round in the mid-1980s. It had evolved into a shotgun slug by the mid-1990s when I met Bill, who was then crowding 80 years old. Wosenitz maintained that at different times deals with Federal Cartridge, Ithaca Gun and Brenneke all fell through or the Venturi Helix would be a household name today. He was still hand-casting himself the last I heard, since demand wasn't high enough to warrant purchasing a swedging machine and no commercial outfit wants to get into the complex casting of interior helix (flutes).

The Venturi Helix projectile before and after firing.

Wosenitz, who had an extensive background in munitions design, was thinking of the .357 magnum pistol bullet when he went to the drawing board originally. When the .357 fell out of favor with law enforcement and the design couldn't be adapted to 9mm because it wouldn't feed adequately, the design was scaled up to 40mm trench mortar dimensions. When he found that the sample his patent attorney wanted would cost $1,000 apiece for testing, he scaled down the model and found that it fit 12-gauge dimensions. "The internal surface has a venturi shape with a convoluted surface of tangent radii on a helix angle, with radial thrust holes, to rotate the projectile in order to establish gyroscopic stability, by

The Venturi Helix — shown here alongside a cutaway version displaying the interior helix fins — started out as an artillery design but the patent model cost so much that it was scaled down to shotgun slug size.

velocity of air through the venturi and holes," Wosenitz explained. In plain language the inside of the tubular projectile has fins or helix that create a venturi effect in the air, creating a vacuum to the rear that keeps the slug stable in flight. The soft lead tube flattens into a doughnut shape upon impact, imparting substantial shock from the 490-grain projectile. He claimed he had a loyal following of handloaders who were routinely achieving MOA groups.

Tony Noblitt came into the business differently than Wosenitz. He was a fanatical shooter with a tinker's bent who happened to live in slug country. Noblitt quit his construction job in 1991 and devoted himself full-ime to marketing his invention — which for my money was the most efficient handloaders' shotgun bullet ever devised — from his Robinson, Illinois, home. Noblitt's Buckbuster Shotgun Bullet was a boat-tailed slug to the point that was not only easy to load but is also very accurate and expanded well. Buckbuster offered three different .68 caliber wadcutter-style bullets that were cold-swaged around a solid copolymer core. They were easily loaded into standard shotgun shotwads that served as sabots in that they contacted the rifling and protected the bore from lead fouling. Roll or folded crimps are fine with the Buckbuster slug.

The 380-grain Hollow Point Keith WadCutter is designed for combat shooters who appreciate lighter recoil. The 435-grain Hollow Point Semi-WadCutter is designed specifically for deer hunting and the 500-grain Flat Point Semi-WadCutter has been used for bear, moose and elk. In the shotwad sabot the ejecta's diameter averages .732 of an inch — which fills any 12-gauge bore. Noblitt's suggested load was a Claybuster 3118-12A wad loaded over 33 grains of IMR 4756 powder in a Remington Premier Target hull. He gets 1,525 feet per second muzzle velocity. A sheet of 15 suggested loads was included with each box of bullets. Unfortunately business logistics got the best of him and the Buckbuster went the way of the dinosaur.

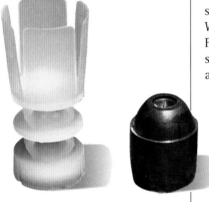

The Buckbuster design featured a Foster-style slug with the rear cavity filled with a polymer to give the slug structural integrity and keep the wad from "leaking" in at setback. A claybird wad was used as a sabot.

what's available now

Ballistic Products, Inc. of Minnesota is absolutely the premier source for slug and/or buckshot handloading components, supplies, manuals, molds, powder, primers, loading tools and virtually anything else the handloader would need or want. They've got plenty of stuff you won't find anywhere else. Precision Reloading of Connecticut is also a leading shotshell component company and recently entered into the shotgun slug business, marketing, among others, the Lyman and Sabot Technologies' HammerHead slugs.

Today there are dozens of slug designs available to handloaders that are sufficiently weird to keep major manufacturers from loading them but that still fill myriad shooting niches and appetites. Lightfield Hybreds,

Barnes EXpander SGS, Gualandi and Chris Young's Collett Cup slugs – all of which are also loaded commercially – are available as projectiles through BPI. The Italian-made Gualandi attached-wad slug, produced commercially by a couple of companies, is available in several sizes through BPI, as is the similarly designed .735-diameter, $1^3/_8$-ounce Thunderbolt. BPI is also an outlet for the 1-ounce .735-diameter 12-gauge Mexican-made Aquila (AQ) slugs, which feature nylon gear-like fins that advertising claims imparts a stabilizing rotation. You can get cast round balls in diameters of .690 (487 grains) and .715 (550 grains) that fit inside conventional shotcups like sabots. BPI markets a frangible Foster-style slug called the Defender in 10-gauge (.660 diameter, 1.5 ounces) and 20 (.615 diameter, $^7/_8$ ounce) and something called an Improved Foster, which is essentially a big wadcutter design with a polished nose that supposedly reduces drag. They are available in 10-, 12- and 28-gauge.

Another small-gauge specialty is the Light Game Slug, an attached wad design that comes in 28-gauge (.505 diameter, 183 grains) and .410 (.375 diameter,

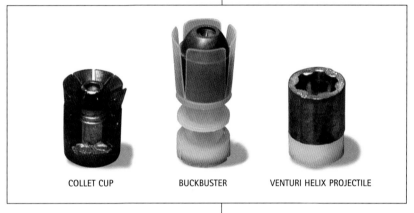

COLLET CUP   BUCKBUSTER   VENTURI HELIX PROJECTILE

The Collet Cup slug, the now-defunct Buckbuster and the Venturi Helix Projectile were and are very effective handloading slugs.

93 grains). Lyman offers an hourglass-shaped slug for handloaders and also sells molds for it. Lee also makes a slug mold. Precision Reloading offers specific recipes for the Sabot Technologies' HammerHead 1-ounce non-discarding sabot slug similar to the Lightfield Commander design. The heavy sabot is a major advantage in that it gives the load a very high ballistic coefficient and can be loaded with a variety of slugs (lead, tungsten, copper, etc.) that make it appealing to special-use applications such as piercing armor, doors or windshields. Regardless of what you load or how you do it, handloading adds a whole new dimension to shotgunning for deer.

appendix – buckshot loads

10-GAUGE BUCKSHOT LOADS

Load			Muzzle	20	30	40	50	60	70
c-Federal Premium	No. 00	velocity	1,100	983	930	882	839	799	762
(18 pellets)		energy	144	113	101	91	82	74	68
c-Winchester Supreme	No. 00	velocity	1,150	1,023	966	915	868	826	787
(18 pellets)		energy	157	122	109	98	88	80	72
c-Federal	No. 1	velocity	1,100	973	916	865	819	777	738
(24 pellets)		energy	108	83	74	66	59	53	48
c-Winchester Classic	No. 4	velocity	1,100	991	918	855	800	749	705
(54 pellets)		energy	62	44	38	33	29	25	22

12-GAUGE BUCKSHOT LOADS

Load			Muzzle	20	30	40	50	60	70
a-Remington Express	No. 000	velocity	1,325	1,176	1,107	1,046	991	941	896
(8 pellets)		energy	275	210	187	167	149	135	122
b-Remington Express	No. 000	velocity	1,225	1,089	1,029	976	928	884	844
(10 pellets)		energy	230	180	161	145	131	119	108
a-Winchester SuperX	No. 000	velocity	1,325	1,176	1,107	1,046	991	941	896
(8 pellets)		energy	275	210	187	167	149	135	122
b-Winchester SuperX	No. 000	velocity	1,225	1,089	1,029	976	928	884	844
(10 pellets)		energy	230	180	161	145	131	119	108
b-Federal Premium	No. 000	velocity	1,225	1,089	1,029	976	928	884	844
(10 pellets)		energy	230	180	161	1451	131	119	108
b-Remington Express	No. 000	velocity	1,221	1,070	1,008	952	902	857	815
(15 pellets)		energy	175	134	119	106	95	85	78
b-Remington Express	No. 000	velocity	1,232	1,078	1,015	959	908	862	820
(10 pellets)		energy	178	136	120	108	97	87	79
a-Remington Hevi-Shot	No. 000	velocity	1,325	1,238	1,188	1,139	1,078	1,031	963
(9 pellets)		energy	303	234	197	170	155	146	130
a-Remington Premier	No. 00	velocity	1,313	1,104	1,070	1,008	952	902	857
(12 pellets)		energy	202	152	134	119	106	95	86
a-Remington Express	No. 00	velocity	1,344	1,164	1,090	1,026	968	917	870
(9 pellets)		energy	212	159	139	123	110	98	89
c-Remington Express	No. 00	velocity	1,125	1,003	948	899	854	812	774
(18 pellets)		energy	151	118	105	94	85	77	70
a-Federal low recoil	No. 00	velocity	1,140	1,023	966	915	868	826	787
(9 pellets)		energy	157	123	109	98	88	80	73
a-Federal Premium	No. 00	velocity	1,290	1,104	1,070	1,008	952	902	857
(12 pellets)		energy	202	152	134	119	106	87	79
b-Federal Premium	No. 00	velocity	1,210	1,070	1,008	952	902	857	815
(15 pellets)		energy	175	134	119	106	95	86	78
c-Federal Premium	No. 00	velocity	1,109	983	930	882	839	799	762
(18 pellets)		energy	144	113	101	91	82	74	68
a-Winchester low recoil	No. 00	velocity	1,125	1,003	948	899	854	812	774
(9 pellets)		energy	151	118	105	95	85	77	70
b-Winchester SuperX	No. 00	velocity	1,210	1,070	1,008	952	902	857	815
(15 pellets)		energy	175	134	119	106	95	86	78
a-Winchester SuperX	No. 00	velocity	1,325	1,164	1,090	1,026	968	917	870
(9 pellets)		energy	212	159	139	123	110	98	89
a-Winchester No. 000	No. 00	velocity	1,313	1,104	1,070	1,008	952	902	857
(15 pellets)		energy	202	152	134	119	106	95	86
c-Winchester SuperX	No. 00	velocity	1,200	1,062	1,001	946	897	852	811
(18 pellets)		energy	172	132	117	105	94	85	77
a-Remington Express	No. 0	velocity	1,212	1,058	996	940	890	844	802
(12 pellets)		energy	157	119	106	94	84	76	68
a-Federal Classic	No. 0	velocity	1,225	1,117	1,047	985	931	881	836
(12 pellets)		energy	177	133	117	103	92	83	75
a-Winchester SuperX	No. 0	velocity	1,275	1,117	1,047	985	931	881	836
(12 pellets)		energy	177	133	117	103	92	83	75
a-Remington Express	No. 1	velocity	1,345	1,149	1,071	1,003	943	889	840
(16 pellets)		energy	159	116	101	88	79	69	62
a-Winchester SuperX	No. 1	velocity	1,250	953	898	849	804	763	726
(16 pellets)		energy	103	80	71	63	57	51	44
a-Winchester Supreme	No. 1	velocity	1,075	1,018	956	901	851	806	714
(20 pellets)		energy	140	104	91	80	71	63	57
b-Winchester SuperX	No. 1	velocity	1,040	925	873	825	784	744	708
(24 pellets)		energy	97	75	67	60	54	49	44
a-Federal Classic	No. 1	velocity	1,250	1,088	1,018	956	901	851	806
(16 pellets)		energy	140	104	91	80	72	64	57
a-Federal Classic	No. 1	velocity	1,085	953	898	849	804	763	726
(20 pellets)		energy	103	80	71	63	57	51	44

appendix – buckshot loads (cont.)

12-GAUGE BUCKSHOT LOADS (cont.)

Load			Muzzle	20	30	40	50	60	70
b-Federal Premium	No. 1	velocity	1,040	925	873	825	784	851	806
(24 pellets)		energy	97	75	67	60	54	49	44
c-Federal Premium	No. 1	velocity	1,110	973	916	865	819	777	738
(24 pellets)		energy	108	83	74	66	59	53	48

16-GAUGE BUCKSHOT LOADS

Load			Muzzle	20	30	40	50	60	70
a-Federal Classic	No. 1	velocity	1,225	1,065	998	938	885	837	793
(12 pellets)		energy	134	100	88	77	69	32	55
a-Winchester SuperX	No. 1	velocity	1,233	1,065	998	938	885	837	793
(12 pellets)		energy	134	100	88	77	69	32	55

20-GAUGE BUCKSHOT LOADS

Load			Muzzle	20	30	40	50	60	70
a-Remington Express	No. 3	velocity	1,200	1,031	955	890	832	781	734
(20 pellets)		energy	76	54	46	40	35	31	27
a-Federal Classic	No. 3	velocity	1,200	1,031	955	890	832	781	734
(20 pellets)		energy	76	54	46	40	35	31	27
b-Federal Classic	No. 2	velocity	1,200	1,036	966	904	849	799	754
(18 pellets)		energy	95	69	60	52	46	41	36
b-Federal Premium	No. 2	velocity	1,175	1,020	951	880	825	777	720
(18 pellets)		energy	93	67	58	50	40	34	30
a-Federal Premium	No. 3	velocity	1,100	931	855	790	740	690	650
(20 pellets)		energy	85	59	38	30	27	22	15
a-Winchester SuperX	No. 3	velocity	1,200	1,031	955	890	832	781	734
(20 pellets)		energy	76	54	46	40	35	31	27
b-Winchester Supreme	No. 3	velocity	1,172	994	924	862	807	758	714
(24 pellets)		energy	70	50	43	38	33	29	26

28-GAUGE BUCKSHOT LOADS

Load			Muzzle	20	30	40	50	60	70
d-RIO	No. 3	velocity	1,357	1,125	1,036	961	894	836	784
(9 pellets)		energy	94	64	55	47	41	35	31

.410-GAUGE BUCKSHOT LOADS

Load			Muzzle	20	30	40	50	60	70
d-Aquila	No. 00	velocity	1,211	1,062	1,001	946	897	852	811
(4 pellets)		energy	172	132	117	105	94	85	77
d-Winchester SuperX	No. 3	velocity	1,300	1,115	978	901	856	817	730
(3 pellets)		energy	88	59	49	38	29	20	13

a- denotes 2.75-inch load   b - denotes 3-inch load   c - denotes 3.5-inch load   d- denotes 2.5-inch load

appendix - slug loads

10-GAUGE FOSTER SLUG LOADS

Load	Type	Wgt (oz)		Muzzle	25	50	75	100	125
c-Federal	Classic rifled	1.75	velocity	1,280	1,160	1,080	1,020	970	*
			energy	2,785	2,295	1,980	1,775	1,605	*
			trajectory	0	0.5	0	-2.3	-6.7	*

12-GAUGE FOSTER SLUG LOADS

Load	Type	Wgt (oz)		Muzzle	25	50	75	100	125
a-Remington	Slugger HV	0.875	velocity	1,800	1,546	1,175	1,043	977	*
			energy	2,751	1,987	1,334	1,089	813	*
			trajectory	0	-0.1	0	-1	-4.1	*
b-Remington	Slugger HV	0.875	velocity	1,875	1,688	1,302	1,184	998	*
			energy	2,989	2,180	1,442	1,121	847	*
			trajectory	0	-0.2	0	-2.3	-7.4	*
a-Remington	Reduced recoil	1	velocity	1,200	1,074	988	926	873	828
			energy	1,397	1,118	946	830	739	665
			trajectory	0	-0.2	0	-2.4	-7.4	-15.2
a-Remington	Slugger	1	velocity	1,680	1,467	1,286	1,144	1,045	974
			energy	2,738	2,088	1,604	1,271	1,059	921
			trajectory	0	-0.2	0	-1.1	-3.8	-8.5
a-Remington	Slugger	1.125	velocity	1,560	1,340	1,175	1,156	977	*
			energy	2,361	1,810	1,340	1,054	926	*
			trajectory	0	-0.1	0	-2.1	-4.8	*
b-Remington	Slugger Mag	1	velocity	1,760	1,690	1,345	1,202	1,075	*
			energy	3,005	2,301	1,753	1,277	1,121	*
			trajectory	0	-0.2	0	-1	-3.4	*
a-Federal	Premium rifled	1	velocity	1,300	1,200	1,110	1,050	1,000	*
			energy	1,645	1,390	1,205	1,070	965	*
			trajectory	0	0.5	0	-2.3	-6.5	*
a-Federal	Classic rifled	1	velocity	1,610	1,460	1,330	1,220	1,140	*
			energy	2,520	2,075	1,725	1,455	1,255	*
			trajectory	0	0.3	0	-1.5	-4.3	*
a-Federal	Classic Mag	1.25	velocity	1,520	1,330	1,260	1,160	1,090	*
			energy	2,805	2,310	1,930	1,645	1,450	*
			trajectory	0	0.3	0	-1.7	-4.9	*
a-Federal	Premium rifled	1	velocity	1,610	1,460	1,330	1,220	1,140	*
			energy	2,520	2,075	1,725	1,455	1,255	*
			trajectory	0	0.3	0	-1.5	-4.3	*
b-Federal	Classic rifled	1.25	velocity	1,600	1,450	1,320	1,210	1,130	*
			energy	3,110	2,555	2,120	1,785	1,540	*
			trajectory	0	0.3	0	-1.5	-4.4	*
a-Winchester	Super X rifled	1	velocity	1,600	1,465	1,161	1,012	953	889
			energy	2,488	2,056	1,310	768	882	768
			trajectory	0	0.4	0	-1.9	-5.9	-12.1
b-Winchester	Super X rifled	1	velocity	1,760	1,602	1,310	1,233	1,040	965
			energy	3,010	2,476	1,667	1,666	1,052	904
			trajectory	0	0.2	0	-1.5	-4.6	-9.7

12-GAUGE FULL-BORE LOADS

Load	Type	Wgt (oz)		Muzzle	25	50	75	100	125
a-Brenneke	Low-recoil	1	velocity	1,246	1,104	1,009	941	886	*
			energy	1,511	1,186	991	862	764	*
			trajectory	0	3.9	4.8	3.6	0	*
a-Brenneke	Hvy Field Mag	1	velocity	1,476	1,310	1,174	1,075	1,002	*
			energy	2,538	2,000	1,606	1,346	1,170	*
			trajectory	0	1.8	2.9	2.4	0	*
a-Brenneke	K.O. slug	1	velocity	1,600	1,377	1,119	1,072	987	*
			energy	2,491	1,845	1,399	1,118	948	*
			trajectory	0	0.3	1.5	1.2	-1	*
b-Brenneke	Super Mag	1	velocity	1,502	1,295	1,136	1,030	995	*
			energy	3,014	2,555	2,120	1,785	1,540	*
			trajectory	0	1.9	3.1	2.5	0	*
b-Brenneke	Black Magic	1.375	velocity	1,502	1,295	1,136	1,030	1,540	*
			energy	3,014	2,555	2,120	1,785	1,540	*
			trajectory	0	1.9	3.1	2.5	0	*
a-Fiocchi	Aeroslug	1	velocity	1,550	1,440	1,340	1,250	1,180	1,110
			energy	2,335	2,020	1,750	1,530	1,345	1,205
			trajectory	0	1.4	2.2	1.8	0	-3.3
a-PMC	Brenneke	1	velocity	1,510	1,460	1,330	1,220	1,140	*
			energy	2,520	2,075	1,725	1,455	1,255	*
			trajectory	0	0.3	0	-1.5	-4.3	*

appendix – slug loads (cont.)

12-GAUGE FULL-BORE LOADS (cont.)

Load	Type	Wgt (oz)		Muzzle	25	50	75	100	125
a-Activ	Premium	1	velocity	1,630	1,507	1,388	1,281	1,190	*
			energy	2,850	2,420	2,054	1,750	1,509	*
			trajectory	0	-0.1	0	-0.4	-2.8	*
a-Activ	Premium	1.25	velocity	1,460	1,349	1,248	1,164	1,098	*
			energy	2,828	2,401	2,055	1,788	1,590	*
			trajectory	0	0.4	0	-1.5	-4.5	*
a-Rottweil	Brenneke Gold	1.38	velocity	1,476	1,286	1,138	1,036	965	*
			energy	2,913	2,209	1,730	1,436	1,244	*
			trajectory	0	1.7	2	1.4	0	*
b-Rottweil	Orig. Brenneke	1.38	velocity	1,502	1,300	1,144	1,037	936	*
			energy	3,017	2,261	1,749	1,438	1,240	*
			trajectory	0	-0.2	0	-1.3	-4.1	*
a-Rottweil	Brenneke MP	1	velocity	1,510	1,300	1,135	1,030	950	*
			energy	2,215	1,640	1,250	1,025	890	*
			trajectory	0	0.1	0	-2	-5.4	*
a-Rottweil	Orig. Brenneke	1	velocity	1,590	1,365	1,190	1,060	965	*
			energy	2,745	2,025	1,540	1,220	1,035	*
			trajectory	0	0.3	1.5	1.2	-1	*

NOTE: No ballistic data available for Challenger, Nitro, Rottweil, Sellier & Belloit, Nitro, Rottweil or Blitz Plus full-bore loads.

12-GAUGE SABOT SLUG LOADS

Load	Type	Wgt (oz)		Muzzle	25	50	75	100	125
a-Winchester	Partition Gold	0.75	velocity	1,900	1,832	1,737	1,689	1,660	1,585
			energy	3,086	2,722	2,579	2,444	2,354	2,148
			trajectory	-0.9	0	0	-0.6	-2	-4.2
a-Winchester	Platinum Tip	0.87	velocity	1,700	1,624	1,551	1,481	1,415	1,353
			energy	2,566	2,342	2,136	1,948	1,791	1,640
			trajectory	-0.9	0	0	-0.9	-2.7	-5.7
a-Winchester	BRI	1	velocity	1,350	1,245	1,122	1,028	988	941
			energy	1,821	1,678	1,259	1,101	975	885
			trajectory	-0.9	0.3	0	-2	-6	-12.2
b-Winchester	BRI	1	velocity	1,400	*	1,151	1,079	1,007	957
			energy	1,958	1,723	1,326	1,177	1,012	914
			trajectory	-0.9	0.2	0	-1.5	-5	-11
a-Winchester	Hi Impact	1	velocity	1,450	*	1,187	*	1,026	972
			energy	2,101	*	1,407	*	1,051	944
			trajectory	0	0.9	2.2	1.9	0	-4.1
b-Winchester	Hi Impact	1	velocity	1,550	*	1,258	*	1,006	1,004
			energy	2,400	*	1,581	*	1,136	1,007
			trajectory	0	0.7	1.7	1.6	0	-3.7
a-Remington	Core-Lokt Ultra	0.88	velocity	1,900	*	1,770	*	1,648	
			energy	3,086	*	2,682	*	2,325	
			trajectory	0	1	1.8	2.1	2.4	1.9
a-Remington	Copper Solid	1	velocity	1,450	1,382	1,319	1,261	1,208	1,161
			energy	2,040	1,854	1,658	1,543	1,416	1,307
			trajectory	0	0.2	0	-1.1	-3.5	-7.4
b-Remington	Copper Solid	1	velocity	1,550	1,476	1,408	1,363	1,283	1,012
			energy	2,331	2,145	1,923	1,709	1,570	1,398
			trajectory	0	1.3	2	1.6	0	-3
a-Remington	BuckHammer	1.25	velocity	1,550	*	1,320	*	1,145	*
			energy	2,935	*	2,177	*	1,600	*
			trajectory	0	0.1	0	-1	-3.6	*
a-Federal	Barnes HV	0.75	velocity	1,900	1,810	1,720	1,640	1,560	1,480
			energy	2,605	2,370	2,140	1,940	1,755	1,585
			trajectory	0	0.9	1.2	1	0	-1.9
a-Federal	Barnes Ex	1	velocity	1,450	1,380	1,320	1,260	1,210	1,160
			energy	2,045	1,860	1,695	1,545	1,420	1,310
			trajectory	0	1.4	2.2	1.8	0	-3.3
b-Federal	Barnes Ex	1	velocity	1,525	1,450	1,390	1,330	1,270	1,210
			energy	2,260	2,055	1,870	1,710	1,560	1,325
			trajectory	0	1.3	2	1.6	0	-3
b-Federal	Premium	1	velocity	1,550	1,440	1,340	1,250	1,180	1,110
			energy	2,335	2,020	1,750	1,530	1,345	1,205
			trajectory	0	1.4	2.2	1.8	0	-3.3
a-Federal	Premium sabot	1	velocity	1,450	1,380	1,260	1,180	1,120	1,070
			energy	2,045	1,775	1,545	1,360	1,215	1,100
			trajectory	0	1.6	2.5	2	0	-3.8
a-Lightfield	Hybred	1.25	velocity	1,402	1,282	1,181	1,100	1,038	988
			energy	2,387	1,997	1,693	1,470	1,308	1,187
			trajectory	0	1.1	2.4	2.1	0	-4.1

appendix – slug loads (cont.)

12-GAUGE SABOT SLUG LOADS (cont.)

Load	Type	Wgt (oz)		Muzzle	25	50	75	100	125
b-Lightfield	Commander	1.25	velocity	1,800	1,638	1,489	1,355	1,239	1,144
			energy	3,274	2,712	2,241	1,856	1,552	1,323
			trajectory	0	2.7	1.23	1.21	0	-2.63
c-Lightfield	Commander	1	velocity	1,850	*	1,576	*	1,357	1,288
			energy	3,444	*	2,403	*	1,689	1,455
			trajectory	0	2.8	1.3	1.2	0	-2.5
a-Lightfield	Lites	1.25	velocity	1,300	*	1,015	*	866	*
			energy	2,049	*	1,330	*	966	*
			trajectory	-1.5	1.33	2.57	2.29	0	-4.38
a-Brenneke	Super Sabot	1.125	velocity	1,407	1,274	1,165	1,080	1,017	*
			energy	2,157	1,770	1,478	1,272	1,127	*
			trajectory	0	1.7	2.9	2.4	0	*
b-Brenneke	Super Sabot	1.125	velocity	1,525	1,376	1,248	1,144	1,065	*
			energy	2,536	2,064	1,697	1,426	1,236	*
			trajectory	0	1.3	2.3	2	0	*
a-Brenneke	KO sabot	1	velocity	1,509	1,344	1,206	1,101	1,024	*
			energy	2,184	1,733	1,395	1,162	1,007	*
			trajectory	0	1.6	2.6	2.2	0	*
b-Brenneke	KO sabot	1	velocity	1,675	1,487	1,325	1,191	1,090	*
			energy	2,686	2,122	1,685	1,361	1,139	*
			trajectory	-2	0	1	0.7	-1.1	*
a-Hornady	H2K Heavy Mag	0.69	velocity	2,000	*	1,850	*	1,788	*
			energy	2,878	*	2,512	*	2,116	*
			trajectory	-1.5	*	0	*	-5.1	*
a-Sauvestre	Ball Fleche	0.91	velocity	1,640	*	*	*	1,235	*
			energy	2,400	*	*	*	1,340	*
			trajectory	-1.5	0	*	*	-1	*
a-Sauvestre	Ball Fleche	0.91	velocity	1,900	*	*	1,420	*	*
			energy	3,230	*	*	1,795	*	*
			trajectory	-1.5	0	*	*	-0.7	*
a-Magnum Perf.	Quik-Shok	1.25	velocity	1,500	1,320	1,170	1,070	1,000	*
			energy	2,457	1,903	1,495	1,309	1,092	*
			trajectory	0	0.3	0	-1.9	-5.2	*

a-denotes 2.75-inch load   b-denotes 3-inch load   c-denotes 3.5-inch load

appendix – slug ballistics

10-GAUGE FOSTER SLUG BALLISTICS

Load	Type	Wgt (oz)		Muzzle	25	50	75	100	125
a-Federal	Classic rifled	0.8	velocity	1,600	1,360	1,180	1,060	990	*
			energy	1,990	1,435	1,075	875	755	*
			trajectory	0	0.3	0	-1.8	-5.4	*
a-Winchester	SuperX	0.8	velocity	1,600	*	1,158	*	950	887
			energy	1,962	*	1,028	*	692	602
			trajectory	0	0.4	0	-2	-5.9	-12.1

16-GAUGE FULL-BORE SLUG BALLISTICS

Load	Type	Wgt (oz)		Muzzle	25	50	75	100	125
a-Rottweil	Brenneke	1	velocity	1,590	1,365	1,190	1,060	975	*
			energy	2,320	1,710	1,300	1,030	875	*
			trajectory	0	1.6	2.6	2.2	0	*
a-Remington	Slugger rifled	0.8	velocity	1,600	*	1,175	*	965	*
			energy	1,989	*	1,072	*	724	*
			trajectory	0	*	0	*	-4.8	*
a-Activ	Premium	1	velocity	1,550	1,432	1,320	1,223	1,144	*
			energy	2,408	2,045	1,738	1,491	1,305	*
			trajectory	0	1.5	2.5	2	0	*

16-GAUGE SABOT SLUG BALLISTICS

Load	Type	Wgt (oz)		Muzzle	25	50	75	100	125
a-Lightfield	Commander	0.9	velocity	1,500	1,344	1,206	1,101	1,024	*
			energy	2,184	1,733	1,395	1,162	1,007	*
			trajectory	0	1.6	2.6	2.2	0	*

appendix – slug ballistics (cont.)

20-GAUGE FOSTER SLUG BALLISTICS

Load	Type	Wgt (oz)		Muzzle	25	50	75	100	125
a-Federal	Classic rifled	0.75	velocity	1,600	1,160	1,270	1,150	1,070	*
			energy	1,865	1,465	1,175	965	835	*
			trajectory	0	0.3	0	-2	-5.9	-12.1
b-Federal	Classic rifled	0.75	velocity	1,680	1,500	1.34	1,210	1,110	*
			energy	2,055	1,640	1,310	1,065	890	*
			trajectory	0	0.2	0	-1.4	-4.4	*
a-Remington	Slugger HV	0.5	velocity	1,800	*	1,321	*	1,037	*
			energy	1,575	*	848	*	523	*
			trajectory	0	*	0	*	-3.6	*
a-Remington	Slugger rifled	0.625	velocity	1,500	*	1,240	*	1,034	*
			energy	1,513	*	931	*	648	*
			trajectory	0	*	0	*	-4.2	*
a-Winchester	SuperX	0.75	velocity	1,600	*	1,160	*	952	889
			energy	1,865	*	981	*	660	575
			trajectory	0	0.3	0	-2	-5.9	-12.1

20-GAUGE FULL-BORE SLUG BALLISTICS

Load	Type	Wgt (oz)		Muzzle	25	50	75	100	125
b-Brenneke	Magnum	1	velocity	1,476	1,322	1,136	1,030	955	*
			energy	2,120	1,701	1,385	1,165	1,016	*
			trajectory	-2	0.4	1.6	1	-1.5	*
b-Rottweil	Orig. Magnum	1	velocity	1,502	1,300	1,144	1,037	936	*
			energy	2,117	1,591	1,239	1,026	888	*
			trajectory	-1.8	0.3	1.5	0.8	-1.3	*
a-Rottweil	Original	0.75	velocity	1,590	1,365	1,190	1,060	976	*
			energy	2,080	1,530	1,165	925	780	*
			trajectory	-2	0.2	1.3	0.6	-1	*
a-Activ	Premium	0.9	velocity	1,570	1,451	1,337	1,238	1,155	*
			energy	2,281	1,937	1,645	1,409	1,227	*
			trajectory	-2	0	1.2	0.6	-0.8	-1

20-GAUGE SABOT SLUG BALLISTICS

Load	Type	Wgt (oz)		Muzzle	25	50	75	100	125
a-Winchester	BRI	0.625	velocity	1,400	*	1,143	*	995	944
			energy	1,162	*	774	*	586	529
			trajectory	0	0.7	1.8	1.7	0	-3.3
a-Winchester	Partition Gold	0.6	velocity	1,900	*	1,721	*	1,555	1,478
			energy	2,084	*	1,709	*	1,396	1,260
			trajectory	0.9	2.2	2.9	2.9	1.9	0
a-Winchester	Platinum Tip	0.6	velocity	1,700	*	1,536	*	1,388	1,321
			energy	1,668	*	1,362	*	1,112	1,008
			trajectory	0	0.2	1.1	1.1	0	-2.2
a-Federal	Premium	0.625	velocity	1,400	1,290	1,190	1,110	1,050	1,000
			energy	1,200	1,010	860	750	670	610
			trajectory	0	1.8	2.8	2.3	0	-4.3
b-Federal	Premium	0.625	velocity	1,450	1,330	1,230	1,140	1,070	1,020
			energy	1,285	1,080	920	795	705	630
			trajectory	0	1.7	2.6	2.2	0	-4
a-Federal	Classic rifled	0.75	velocity	1,600	1,420	1,270	1,150	1,070	*
			energy	1,865	1,465	1,175	965	835	*
			trajectory	0	0.3	0	-1.6	-4.8	*
b-Federal	Classic rifled	0.75	velocity	1,680	1,500	1,340	1,210	1,110	*
			energy	2,055	1,640	1,310	1,065	890	*
			trajectory	0	0.2	0	-1.4	-4.4	*
b-Federal	Barnes X	0.75	velocity	1,450	1,380	1,320	1,260	1,200	1,150
			energy	1,515	1,375	1,250	1,140	1,040	960
			trajectory	0	1.5	2.3	1.8	0	-3.3
a-Lightfield	Hybred	0.93	velocity	1,475	1,381	1,295	1,218	1,153	1,097
			energy	1,850	1,621	1,426	1,262	1,129	1,024
			trajectory	0	0.7	1.8	1.7	0	-3.3
a-Remington	Copper Solid	0.625	velocity	1,500	*	1,360	*	1,240	*
			energy	1,444	*	1,187	*	986	*
			trajectory	0	*	0	*	-3.1	*
a-Remington	Core-Lokt Ultra	260	velocity	1,900	*	1,750	*	1,615	*
			energy	2,084	*	1,774	*	1,506	*
			trajectory	0	*	2	*	2.7	0

appendix – slug regulations

State	County level restrictions	Buckshot, slugs	Buckshot, centerfire, slugs	Slugs only	Centerfire, slugs
Alabama	x		x		
Alaska			x		
Arizona					x
Arkansas	x		x		
California	x		x		
Colorado					x
Connecticut	x				x
Delaware		x			
Florida			x		
Georgia	x		x		
Hawaii			x		
Idaho			x		
Illinois				x	
Indiana				x	
Iowa				x	
Kansas					x
Kentucky					x
Louisiana			x		
Maine			x		
Maryland	x		x		
Massachusetts		x			
Michigan	x		x		
Minnesota	x				x
Mississippi			x		
Missouri					x
Montana	x		x		
Nebraska					x
Nevada					x
New Hampshire	x		x		
New Jersey		x			
New Mexico					x
New York	x				x
North Carolina			x		
North Dakota	x				x
Ohio				x	
Oklahoma					x
Oregon			x		
Pennsylvania			x		
Rhode Island		x			
South Carolina			x		
South Dakota					x
Tennessee					x
Texas			x		
Utah			x		
Vermont			x		
Virginia	x		x		
Washington			x		
West Virginia					x
Wisconsin	x		x		
Wyoming			x		

Information from Winchester-Olin and state fish & wildlife department hunting regulations

appendix - products

Shotguns

Benelli-Stoeger-Franchi
17603 Indian Head Highway
Accokeek, MD 20607
301-283-6981
www.benelliusa.com
www.franchiusa.com

Beretta USA
17601 Beretta Drive
Accokeek, MD 20607
301-283-2191
www.berettausa.com

Browning
One Browning Place
Morgan, UT 84050
801-876-2711
www.browning.com

Charles Daly
K.B.I. Inc.
P.O. Box 6625
Harrisburg, PA 17112
866-DALYGUN
www.charlesdaly.com

European American Armory
P.O. Box 1299
Sharpes, FL 32959
321-639-4842
www.eaacorp.com

Heckler & Koch, Inc.
(Fabarms)
21480 Pacific Blvd.
Sterling, VA 22170-8903
703-450-1900
www.hecklerkoch-usa.com

Ithaca Gun
420 North Walpole Street
Upper Sandusky, OH 43351
877-648-4222
www.ithacagun.com

Marlin Firearms Co.
100 Kenna Drive
North Haven, CT 06473
203-239-5621
www.marlinfirearms.com

New England Firearms Co., Inc.
(also H&R 1871)
Industrial Rowe
Gardner, MA 01440
978-632-9393

O.F. Mossberg & Sons, Inc.
7 Grasso Avenue
North Haven, CT 06473
203-230-5300
www.mossberg.com

Remington Arms Co., Inc.
870 Remington Drive
P.O. Box 700
Madison, NC 27025-0700
800-243-9700
www.remington.com

Savage Arms, Inc.
118 Mountain Road
Suffield, CT 06078
800-235-1821
www.savagearms.com

SKB Shotguns
4325 South 120th Street
Omaha, NE 68137
800-752-2767
www.skbshotguns.com

Tar-Hunt Slug Guns
101 Dogtown Road
Bloomsburg, PA 17815
570-784-6368
www.tar-hunt.com

Traditions Performance Firearms
1375 Boston Post Road
Old Saybrook, CT 06475
860-388-4656
www.traditionsfirearms.com

U.S. Repeating Arms
(Winchester Firearms)
275 Winchester Avenue
Morgan, UT 84050-9333
801-876-3440
www.winchester-guns.com

Weatherby, Inc.
3100 El Camino Real
Atascadero, CA 93422
800-227-2016
www.weatherby.com

Ammunition

Aquila
c/o Centurion Ordnance Inc.
11614 Rainbow Ridge
Helotes, TX 78023
210-695-4602
www.aguilaammo.com

Brenneke of America
P.O. Box 1481
Clinton, IA 52733
800-753-9733
www.brennekeusa.com

Dynamit-Nobel/RWS
81 Ruckman Road
Closter, NJ 07624
201-767-1995
www.dnrws.com

Federal Cartridge Company
900 Ehlen Drive
Anoka, MN 55303
763-323-3834
www.federalcartridge.com

Fiocchi of America
6930 Fremont Road
Ozark, MO 65721
417-725-4118
www.fiocchiusa.com

Hevi-Shot
EnvironMetal, Inc.
1307 Clark Mill Road
Sweet Home, OR 97386
541-367-3522
Hevishot@aol.com

Hornady Manufacturing
3625 Old Potash Highway
Grand Island, NE 68803
308-382-1390
www.hornady.com

Kent Cartridge
10000 Zigor Road
Kearneysville, WV 25430
888-311-KENT
www.kentgamebore.com

Lightfield Ammunition
P.O. Box 162
Adelphia, NJ 07710
732-462-9200
www.lightfield-ammo.com

Nitro Company Ammunition
7560 Newkirk Rd.
Mountain Grove, MO 65711
417-746-4600
www.nitrocompany.com

PMC Ammunition
P.O. Box 62508
Boulder City, NV 89006
702-294-0025
www.pmcammo.com

Polywad Shotgun Shells
P.O. Box 7916
Macon, GA 31209
800-998-0669
www.polywad.com

Remington, Inc.
870 Remington Drive
P.O. Box 700
Madison, NC 27025-0700
800-243-9700
www.remington.com

Sellier & Bellot, USA
P.O. Box 7307
Shawnee Mission, KS 66207
800-960-2422
ceg@sb-usa.com

Winchester/Olin
427 N. Shamrock Street
East Alton, IL 62024-1174
618-258-2204
www.winchester.com

Wolf Performance Ammunition
2201 E. Winston Road, Suite K
Anaheim, CA 92806
888-757-WOLF
www.wolfammo.com

Choke Tubes, Barrels

Anderson Custom
170 Antioch Road
Batesville, AR 72501
866-307-0500
keith@customshotguns.com

Angle Porting
By Ballistic Specialties
P.O. Box 2401
Batesville, AR 72503
800-276-2550
www.angleport.com

Bansner's Custom Gunsmithing
261 East Main Street
Adamstown, PA 19501
717-484-2370

Briley Manufacturing
1230 Lumpkin Road
Houston, TX 77043
800-331-5718
www.briley.com

Carlson's
P.O. Box 162
Atwood, KS 67730
785-626-3700

Cation
(Sniper choke tubes)
2341 Alger Street
Troy, MI 48083
810-689-0658
cation@mich.com

Clear View Products
3021 N. Portland Road
Oklahoma City, OK 73107
405-943-9222

Colonial Arms
1109C Singleton Dr.
Selma, AL 36702
800-949-8088
www.colonialarms.com

Comp-N-Choke
925 Waynesboro Highway
Sylvania, GA 30467
888-875-7906
www.comp-n-choke.com

Hastings Barrels
KEBCO LLC
PO Box 300
Hanover, PA 17331
717-524-5301
www.hastingsbarrels.com

Haydel's Game Calls
5018 Hazel Jones Road
Bossier City, LA 71111
800-HAYDELS
www.haydels.com

Kick's Industries
925 Waynesboro Highway
Sylvania, GA 30467
888-587-2779
www.kicks-ind.com

Marble Arms/Poly-Choke
P.O. Box 111
Gladstone, MI 49837
906-428-3710

Nu-Line Guns
1053 Caulks Hill Road
Harvester, MO 63304
636-441-4500
nulineguns@nulineguns.com

Patternmaster
6431 North Taos Road
Scott City, KS 67871
620-872-3022

Rhino Chokes
21890 NE Highway 27
Williston, FL 32696
800-226-3613
rhinoman@atlantic.net

Seminole Gunworks
3049 US Route 1
Mims, FL 32754
800-980-3344
www.seminolegun.com

Stan Baker Barrels
10000 Lake City Way
Seattle, WA 98125
206-522-4575

Trulock Chokes
102 E. Broad Street
Whigham, GA 31797
800-293-9402
www.trulockchokes.com

Wright's, Inc.
4591 Shotgun Alley
Pinckneyville, IL 62274
618-357-8933
www.wrightschokes.com

Organizations

National Reloading Manufacturers Association
One Centerpoint Drive 300
Lake Oswego, OR 97035

National Rifle Association
11250 Waples Mill Road
Fairfax, VA 22030
703-267-1000
www.nra.org

Sporting Arms & Ammunition Manufacturers Institute (SAAMI)
11 Mile Hill Road
Flintlock Ridge Office Center
Newton, CT 06470
203-426-1320
www.saami.org

Gun Care Products

Beretta Gallery
718 Madison Ave.
New York, NY 10021
212-319-3235
www.berettausa.com

Birchwood Casey
7900 Fuller Rd.
Eden Prairie, MN 55344
800-328-6156
www.birchwoodcasey.com

BoreSnake
GunMate
P.O. Box 1720
Oregon City, OR 97045
503-655-2837

Bore Tech Inc.
2950 N. Advance Lane
Colmar, PA 18915
215-997-9689
www.boretech.com

Break-Free Inc.
An Armor Holdings
13386 International Pkwy
Jacksonville, FL 32218
800-428-0588
www.break-free.com

Chem-Pak Inc.
242 Corning Way
Martinsburg, WV 25401
800-336-9828
www.chem-pak.com

Choke Shine
G.E.M.S. Inc.
33717 Hwy 23
Collins, GA 30421
888-507-8762
www.chokeshine.com

Corrosion Technologies
P.O. Box 551625
Dallas, TX 75355-1625
800-638-7361
corrosnx@ix.netcom.com

J. Dewey Rods
P.O. Box 2104
Southbury, CT 06488
203-264-3064

DSX Products
M.S.R. Inc.
P.O. Box 1372
Sterling, VA 20167-1372
800-822-0258

Du-Lite Corp.
171 River Rd.
Middletown, CT 06457
860-347-2505

EEZOX Inc.
P.O. Box 772
Waterford, CT 06385
800-462-3331

Flitz International
821 Mohr Ave.
Waterford, WI 53185
800-558-8611
www.flitz.com

Free Gun Cleaner
Frigon Guns
1605 Broughton Rd.
Clay Center, KS 67432
785-632-5607

Golden Bore Gun Care
Termark International
200 W. 17th St.
Cheyenne, WY 82001
888-483-7677
goldenbore@usa.net

H&R Outdoors
914 Artic St.
Bridgeport, CT 06608
888-761-4250

Hoppes
Div. of Michaels of Oregon
Airport Industrial Mall
Coatesville, PA 19320
610-384-6000
www.hoppes.com

The Inhibitor
Van Patten Industries
PO Box 6694
Rockford, IL 61125
815-332-4812
www.theinhibitor.com

International Lubrication Labs
1895 East 56 Rd.
Lecompton, KS 66050
785-887-6004

Iosso Products
1485 Lively Blvd.
Elk Grove, IL 60007
847-437-8400
www.iosso.com

Kleen-Bore Inc.
16 Industrial Pkwy
Easthampton, MA 01027
800-445-0301

Mpro7 Gun Care
Windfall Inc.
P.O. Box 54988
225 W. Deer Valley Rd. #4
Phoenix, AZ 85078
800-YES-4MP7

Ms Moly Ballistic Conditioner
1952 Knob Rd.
Burlington, WI 53105
800-264-4140

MTM Molded Products
3370 Obco Court
Dayton, OH 45413
513-890-7461

Neco
536 C. Stone Rd.
Benicia, CA 94510
707-747-0897

Otis Technology
P.O. Box 582
Lyons Falls, NY 13368
800-OTISGUN
www.otisgun.com

Outers
P.O. Box 38
Onalaska, WI 54650
608-781-5800

Ox-Yoke Originals
34 West Main St.
Milo, ME 04463
207-943-7351

Peak Enterprises
79 Bailey Dr.
Newman, GA 30263
770-253-1397
tpeak@west.ga.net

Prolix
div. Pro-ChemCo
P.O. Box 1348
Victorville, CA 92393-1348
760-243-3129
prolix@accex.net

Pro-Shot Products
P.O. Box 763
Taylorsville, IL 62568
217-824-9133
www.proshotproducts.com

ProTec International
1747 Bartlett Rd.
Memphis, TN 38134
800-843-5649 ext. 101
sales@proteclubricants.com

Rapid Rod
ATSKO Inc.
2664 Russell St.
Orangeburg, SC 29115
800-845-2728
info@atsko.com

Rig Products
56 Coney Island Dr.
Sparks, NV 89509
775-359-4451

Rusteprufe Labs
1319 Jefferson Ave.
Sparta, WI 54656
608-269-4144
rusteprufe@centurytel.net

Salvo Industries
5173 N. Douglas Fir Rd.
Calabasas, CA 91302
818-222-2276
jacob@ammotech.com

Sentry Solutions
111 Sugar Hill Rd.
Contoocook, NH 03229
603-746-5687
bwc@sentrysolutions.com

Shooters Choice Gun Care
c/o Ventco Industries
15050 Berkshire Industrial Pkwy
Middlefield, OH 44062

440-834-8888
shooters@shooter-choice.com

Sinclair International
2330 Wayne Haven St.
Fort Wayne, IN 46803
260-493-1858
www.sinclairintl.com

Slip 2000
Superior Products
355 Mandela Pkwy
Oakland, CA 94607
707-585-8329
www.slip2000.com

Sports Care Products
P.O. Box 589
Aurora, OH 44202
888-428-8840

TDP Industries
606 Airport Rd.
Doylestown, PA 18901
215-345-8687

Tetra Gun Care
FTI Inc.
8 Vreeland Rd.
Florham Park, NJ 07932
973-443-0004

300-Below Cryogenic Tempering
2999 Parkway Drive
Decatur, IL 62526
217-423-3070
www.300below.com

Thunder Products
P.O. Box H
San Jose, CA 95151
408-270-4200

Tipton
c/o Battenfeld Technologies
5885 West Van Horn Tavern Road
Columbia, MO 65203
877-509-9160
www.battenfeldtechnologies.com

White Lightning
Leisure Innovations
1545 Fifth Industrial Ct.
Bay Shore, NY 11706
800-390-9222

Reloading Equipment

Ballistic Products Inc.
P.O. Box 293
Hamel, MN 55340
763-494-9237
www.ballisticproducts.com

Battenfeld Technologies
5885 West Van Horn Tavern Road
Columbia, MO 65203
877-509-9160
www.battenfeldtechnologies.com

Brownells, Inc.
200 South Front St.
Montezuma, IA 50171
641-623-5401
www.brownells.com

Dillon Precision
8009 E. Dillon's Way
Scottsdale, AZ 85260
602-948-8009
www.dillonprecision.com

Hornady Mfg.
Box 1848
Grand Island, NE 68802
308-382-1390

Lee Precision
4275 Highway U
Hartford, WI 53027
262-673-3075

Lyman Products
475 Smith Street
Middletown, CT 06457
860-632-2020
www.lymanproducts.com

MEC
Mayfield Engineering
715 South St.
Mayville, WI 53050
920-387-4500
www.mecreloaders.com

Midway USA
5885 West Van Horn Tavern Road
Columbia, MO 65203
1-800-243-3220
www.midwayusa.com

Ponsness/Warren
768 Ohio St.
Rathdrum, ID 83858
208-687-2231
bsteele@reloaders.com

Precision Reloading
P.O. Box 122
Stafford Springs, CT 06076-0122
860-684-5680
www.precisionreloading.com

RCBS
P.O. Box 39
Onalaska, WI 54650
800-635-7656
www.outers-guncare.com

Spolar Power Load
2273 S. Vista B-2
Bloomington, CA 92316
800-227-9667
www.spolargold.com

Powders, Components

Accurate Arms
5891 Highway 230 West
McEwen, TN 37101
800-416-3006
www.accuratepowder.com

ADCO/NobelSport
4 Draper St.
Woburn, MA 01801
781-935-1799
www.adcosales.com

Alaskan Cartridge
RR2 Box 192F
Hastings, NE 68901-9408
402-463-3415

Alliant Powder Co.
P.O. Box 4
State Rte. 114
Radford, VA 21141-0096
800-276-9337
dick-quesenberry@atk.com

Ball Powder Propellant
St. Marks Powder
P.O. Box 222
St. Marks, FL 32355
850-577-2273
srfaintich@stm.gd-ots.com

Ballistic Products, Inc.
P.O. Box 293
Hamel, MN 55340
763-494-9237
www.ballisticproducts.com

Barnes Bullets Inc.
750 North 2600 West
Lindon, UT 84042
801-756-4222
www.barnesbullets.com

Claybuster Wads
C&D Special Products
309 Sequoya Dr.
Hopkinsville, Ky 42240
502-885-8088
dmac@spis.net

Clean Shot Technologies
21218 St. Andrews Blvd #504
Boca Raton, FL 33433
888-419-2073
cleanshot@aol.com

Duster Wads
Micro Technologies
1405 Laukant St.
Reedsburg, WI 53959
888-438-7837

Hodgdon Powder
6231 Robinson Street
Shawnee Mission, KS 66201
913-362-9455
info@hodgdon.com

Lawrence Brand Shot
Metalico-Granite City
1200 16th St.
Granite City, IL 62040
618-451-4400

Lee Precision
4275 Highway U
Hartford, WI 53027
262-673-3075

Lightfield Ammunition
P.O. Box 162
Adelphia, NJ 07710
732-462-9200
www.lightfield-ammo.com

Lyman Products
475 Smith Street
Middletown, CT 06457
860-632-2020
www.lymanproducts.com

Polywad
P.O .Box 7916
Macon, GA 31209
800-998-0669
www.polywad.com

RamShot Powders
c/o Western Powders
P.O. Box 158
Yellowstone Hill
Miles City, MT 59301
800-497-1007
powder@midrivers.com

Reloading Specialties
52901 265th Ave.
Pine Island, MN 55963
507-356-8500

Sabot Technologies Inc.
P.O. Box 189
Alum Bank, PA 15521-0189
877-704-4868
www.sabottechnologies.com
www.SlugsRus.com

Vihtavuori/Lapua
Kalton-Pettibone
1241 Ellis St.
Bensenville, IL 60106
800-683-0464
jbolda@kaltron.com

Other Contacts

American Gunsmithing Institute
1325 Imola Avenue, W. 504
Napa, CA 94559
707-253-0462
www.americangunsmith.com

Second Skin Camo
3434 Buck Mt. Road
Roanoke, VA 24014
540-774-9248
www.trebark.com

300-Below Cryogenic Tempering
2999 Parkway Drive
Decatur, IL 62526
217-423-3070
www.300below.com

Scopes, Sights

ADCO Sales
4 Draper Street
Woburn, MA 01801
800-775-3687
www.adcosales.com

Aimpoint
7702 Leesburg Pike
Falls Church, VA 22043
877-246-7646
www.aimpoint.com

AO Sight Systems
XS Sight Systems
2401 Ludelle Street
Fort Worth, TX 76105
888-744-4880
www.xssights.com

BSA Sport
3911 SW 47th Avenue, Suite 914
Ft. Lauderdale, FL 33314
954-581-2144
www.bsaoptics.com

Burris Company
331 East 8th Street
Greeley, CO 80631-9559
970-356-1670
www.burrisoptics.com

Bushnell Performance Optics
(also Tasco)
9200 Cody
Overland Park, KS 66214
800-423-3537
www.bushnell.com
www.tasco.com

Deutsche Optik
P.O. Box 601114
San Diego, CA 92160-1114
800-225-9407
www.deutscheoptik.com

Fujinon Inc.
10 High Point Drive
Wayne, NJ 07470
973-633-5600
www.fujinon.jp.co

HiViz Shooting Systems
1841 Heath Parkway, Suite 1
Fort Collins, CO 80524
800-589-4315
www.hivizsights.com

Hunter Wicked Optics
3300 W. 71st Avenue
Westminster, CO 80030-5303
800-676-4868
www.huntercompany.com

Ironsighter Company
P.O. Box 85070
Westland, MI 48185
734-326-8731
www.ironsighter.com

Leatherwood/Hi-Lux Optics
2535 West 237th Street, Suite 106
Torrance, CA 90505
310-257-8142
www.leatherwoodoptics.com

Legacy Sports International
(Nikko-Stirling Scopes)
206 South Union Street
Alexandria, VA 22314
703-548-4837
www.legacysports.com

Leupold & Stevens
14400 Northwest Greenbriar Parkway
Beaverton, OR 97006
503-646-9171
www.leupold.com

Millett Sights
16131-K Gothard Street
Huntington Beach, CA 92647
714-842-5575
www.millettsights.com

Nikon Sport Optics
1300 Walt Whitman Road
Melville, NY 11747
631-547-4200
www.nikonusa.com

Pentax USA
35 Inverness Drive East
Englewood, CO 80112
800-877-0155
www.pentaxlightseeker.com

Schmidt & Bender
Am Grossacker 42
Biebertal
Hessen Germany 35444
011-49-6409-8115-0
www.schmidt-bender.de

Shepherd Enterprises
2920 North 240th Street
Waterloo, NE 68069
www.shepherdscopes.com

Sightron Inc
100 Jeffrey Way, Suite A
Youngsville, NC 27596
919-562-3000
www.sightron.com

Swarovski Optik North America
2 Slater Road
Cranston, RI 02920
401-734-1800
www.swarovskioptik.com

Swift Instruments
952 Dorchester Avenue
Boston, MA 02125
617-436-2960
www.swift-optics.com

Thompson Center Company
P.O. Box 5002
Rochester, NH 03867
603-332-2394
www.tcarms.com

Trijicon Inc
49385 Shafer Avenue
Wixom, MI 48393
800-338-0563
www.trijicon.com

TRUGLO Inc.
13745 Neutron Road
Dallas, TX 75244
972-774-0300
www.truglo.com

Ultra Dot
6304 Riverside Drive
Yankeetown, FL 34498-0362
352-447-2255
www.ultradotusa.com

U.S. Optics Technologies
5900 Dale Street
Buena Park, CA 90621
714-994-4901
www.usoptics.com

Williams Gun Sight
7389 Lapeer Road
Davison, MI 48423
800-530-9028
www.williamsgunsight.com

Carl Zeiss Optics
13005 North Kingston Avenue
Chester, VA 23836
800-441-3005
www.zeiss.com

Mounts, Rings

Aimtech Mount Systems
P.O. Box 223
Thomasville, GA 31799-0223
229-226-4313
www.aimtech-mounts.com

B-Square
2708 Saint louis Avenue
Fort Worth, TX 76110
800-433-2909
www.b-square.com

Burris Company
331 East 8th Street
Greeley, CO 80631-9559
970-356-1670
www.burrisoptics.com

Custom Quality Mounts
345 West Girard Street
Madison Heights, MI 48071
248-585-1616

Kwik-Site Company
5555 Treadwell

Wayne, MI 48184
734-326-1500
www.kwiksitecorp.com

Leupold & Stevens
14400 Northwest Greenbriar Parkway
Beaverton, OR 97006
503-646-9171
www.leupold.com

Millett Sights
16131-K Gothard Street
Huntington Beach, CA 92647
714-842-5575
www.millettsights.com

Redfield Mounts
P.O. Box 39
Onalaska, WI 54650
608-781-5800
www.redfield-mounts.com

Simmons Mounts
P.O. Box 39
Onalaska, WI 54650
608-781-5800
www.simmons-mounts.com

Stoney Point Products
1822 North Minnesota Street
New Ulm, MN 56073-0234
507-354-3360
www.stoneypoint.com

Talley Manufacturing
P.O. Box 821
Glenrock, WY 82637
307-436-8724
www.talleyrings.com

Warne Scope Mounts
9057 Southeast Jannsen Road
Clackamas, OR 97015
503-657-5590
www.warnescopemounts.com

Weaver Mounts
P.O. Box 39
Onalaska, WI 54650
608-781-5800
www.weaver-mounts.com

Wideview Scope Mounts
13535 South Highway 16
Rapid City, SD 57702
605-341-3220

Index

Photo Credits:

Courtesy Remington: 12, 28(top),
    30(bottom), 33(top), 43(bottom);
Courtesy Quaker Boy Calls: 15(bottom);
Courtesy Brenneke USA: 16;
Courtesy Winchester-Olin: 24(top);
Courtesy Howard Communications:
    33(bottom);
Courtesy Federal Ammunition: 43(top);
Chris Young: 106.